10 Mistakes of Risk Management and How to Avoid Them

by

Rai Chowdhary

Ten Mistakes of Risk Management and How to Avoid Them

Copyright 2007

by

Rai Chowdhary

Cataloging-in-Publication Data

Chowdhary, Rai
Ten Mistakes of Risk Management and How to Avoid Them

p.   cm.

Risk Management. 2. Organizational Change. 3. Business Skills
4. Problem Solving.
I. Author. II. Title.

978-0-9801756-0-8   HD 61 K28 2008   658.155

TEAM 2000
8760A, Research Blvd., #418
Austin, Texas 78758

Printed in the United States of America

Table of Contents

Dedicated to my mother

Dedicated to my mother

What This Book is About

There are few parallels to the thrill of performing a high wire act. Beyond imagination, one has to ask if success will be a matter of choice or chance?

The frontiers of risk often recede faster than our advances in managing risk. Mistakes, it is said, are the best way to learn. However, they can be *expensive, and very time consuming.* Besides, they are not taken kindly in the business world. Therefore, to be successful, we will need to do three things. They are:

- Learn from past, and others' mistakes.
- Live in the present using the principles and practice of Risk Management, and
- Lead into the future with foresight.

Together these will provide a firm foundation for success. Risk taking is a must: *reckless risk taking is not.* The purpose of this book is to increase your understanding of the mistakes we make in Risk Management. This will be accomplished by:

- ❖ Studying disasters and failures from the past.
- ❖ Examining Ten Mistakes that lead to erroneous thinking and actions.
- ❖ Probing the causes of such mistakes, and
- ❖ Exploring simple tools and techniques that anyone can use to prevent these mistakes. An in depth statistical approach is beyond the scope of this book.

I am ready to work with you, are you ready to begin the journey?

How This Book is Organized

This book is organized in three parts. Part I presents significant events from the last 30 years, and poses some questions for you to work on. Part II looks at Ten Mistakes we humans make, and Part III focuses on what you can do to avoid these mistakes.

Study each of the events from Part I and ask yourself if they were really accidents *(unexpected)*, acts of God, or events just waiting to happen. Self-assessment questions in this section involve quick thinking and judgment calls; I encourage you to answer these before you proceed to the rest of the book. They will work as eye openers, and you will refer back to them as you read subsequent sections. I recommend you book mark these pages.

Part II looks at the Ten Mistakes, discussing one mistake at a time. Risk analysis requires *more* rational thinking than we normally do. That is the reason we should understand the factors that can lead to *irrational* thinking and behaviors. At the end of Part II, I present some exercises based on real situations - to sharpen your skills at spotting the mistakes, and segue for understanding human behavior in the next section.

Part III begins with a discovery of the human dimension, and then provides tools and techniques as antidotes. All of them are included in this chapter to maintain continuity and allow you to see how one antidote can be useful against several mistakes. A table for mapping the antidotes to the Ten Mistakes is provided for you to reinforce understanding. This part culminates with 30 trends (or events) to watch going forward. They contain seeds of potentially far reaching global events down the road.

Appendices A through D contain additional tools used in improving your ability to manage risks. The examples in the book, and the seven case studies at the end are from actual applications (or adaptations from actual events). True names of the participants and companies have been changed in most cases to maintain confidentiality.

Lastly, I encourage you to wear the hat of a perennial student. The more you learn, the more acumen you will build, and realize how much there is to know!

Acknowledgements

Assisting people in all walks of life to *discover* the risks they face, and *how to* manage the same has become a passion for me over the last eight years. An important pre-requisite for being successful is to know how to prevent failure or disaster. This doesn't mean one has to become paralyzed by the fear of risk to the point of inaction. Smart risk taking is a journey; it requires a different way of thinking, and proficiency in use of several tools and techniques. I have been on this journey for decades, and worked with a very distinguished and diverse group of people. Some have been my mentors, some my friends, associates, and teachers. In creating this book, all have contributed to varying extents.

The challenge of assembling the experiences and knowledge in this work proved more daunting than I had imagined. I started writing this book in 2004, based on personal experiences, and bits and pieces of the myriad mistakes that people make while dealing with risk. Based on the observations I developed a methodology for managing risk. Putting it all together into a package started much later as I saw increasing numbers of professionals fall short in their ability to foresee and tackle failures *before* they occurred. Ashok Khandkar, CEO of Amedica, was among the rare executives who saw the benefits of these approaches early, and encouraged his executive staff to adopt these techniques in their operations.

I am indebted to Dr. Richard Grant of Austin, Texas, for his mentoring and guidance on linking the temperament types with risk management. He has been a source of inspiration and ideas that were crucial in completing this work.

Thanks are also due to Prof. H. C. Patel of National Center for

Quality Management (Mumbai, India) for his support and encouragement.

Without help from Cherie Nicholson, I would not have been able to complete the interviews and research needed to finish the book. I also thank Aura Stewart, and Kathy Flories who helped align my writing with the key messages I wanted to convey.

Last but not least, I am grateful to my wife Kiran Chowdhary for her patience, support, and gentle reminders to stay the course.

Rai Chowdhary

Introduction

One day during the summer of 1989, while we were living in Austin, I had come home from work and was playing with my daughters. Pujeeta, the elder one, was four years old, and Meeta was little over one.

Our rented house was located in a nice cul-de-sac of a quiet neighborhood. The sun had set, and twilight was fading away into the night when I noticed a dim glow on the curtains of our northern windows. Thinking the neighbors had turned on the lights, I didn't pay much attention and went back to playing with my kids; however, in a matter of minutes the glow grew brighter and appeared to flicker. Curiosity drove me to peek behind the curtains. To my horror, I saw the neighbor's house in flames.

Our house, about twelve feet from theirs, had only a wooden fence separating us, and that too had started to burn. The grass between our house and the fence was not on fire yet, and I could tell the wind god did not look favorably upon us that day; a southerly breeze was swaying the flames toward our house.

Knowing that the houses in this neighborhood were primarily of wood construction, I yelled as loud as I could for everyone to get out of the house. Hastily, I picked up Meeta, grabbed Pujeeta by her arm, and instructed my wife and mother to follow. They wanted to gather some belongings, impatiently I yelled again, as loud as I could, "Get out, right now!"

We ran out into the cul-de-sac and saw the flames leaping upwards, devouring the neighbor's house amidst smoke and crackling sounds. A small crowd had gathered, yet, none of the onlookers could do anything except watch helplessly. Pieces of the roof fell, and more flames spread southward. The grass between our house and the fence was now on fire, and, in a matter of minutes, it seemed the north walls of our house would begin to burn as well.

A few feet away, Mr. Jones stood in his underwear, holding his three-month-old baby. Tears streamed down his face. Sobbing and in shock, neighbors surrounded him and tried to console him.

The fire truck arrived before too long, and the firemen got to work quickly. They doused the flames and brought the fire under control. In order to prevent the fire from spreading, they pointed their hoses on our house and the fence. Our neighbor's house had completely burned, except for parts of the charred frame and roof. The fire had damaged parts of our roof, and the north wall. It had all happened so quickly. I estimate the time from noticing the dim glow on the curtains to the time the flames consumed the neighbor's house was only about five or six minutes. Yet, those few minutes seemed like eternity.

After the fire trucks left, the whole story gradually emerged. Mr. Jones had put his son to bed and began cooking some French fries as part of his dinner. A short time later, he heard his son crying and went to see him. After calming him, he put him back to sleep in the crib. Meanwhile, he forgot about the fries and went to take a shower. Shortly thereafter, he heard the fire alarm.

Suddenly remembering the fries he ran to the kitchen through smoke filled rooms and hallways only to find the kitchen burning. For a few moments, he fumbled to find the fire extinguisher but couldn't. The flames and smoke spread with frightening speed, so he ran to the bedroom coughing and choking, picked up his son and escaped the inferno from a window. Meanwhile, Mrs. Applegate from across the street had noticed flames coming out from the kitchen window and called 911.

Shortly after this incident, I researched statistics on house fires and found that:

- ❖ Cooking was the leading cause of fire incidents in residences.[1]
- ❖ The location and presence of fire alarms was rather arbitrary.[1]
- ❖ Fire extinguishers were not mandatory equipment in homes.

Recent research and data show that:

- Over 350,000 residential fires[3] occurred in the U.S. during 2002, amounting to 40 fires/hour. Of these, about 156,000 were kitchen fires.[1]
- Kitchen fires peaked between 6 and 7 p.m.[1]
- The primary cause of kitchen fires was unattended equipment, and the material that ignited first was grease or oil.[1]
- Unattended cooking led all causes of home cooking fires.[1,3]
- Smoke alarms were reported to be present in 95% of the houses based on a 2004 phone survey; however, about a quarter of these were non-functional, mainly due to dead batteries or disconnected cables.[3]

These problems are not limited to the U.S. alone. Further investigation showed as follows:

- 56% of the houses in U.K. did not have functional smoke alarms in 2003.[2]
- Over 10,000 house fires occurred in Australia during 2000, 30% of which started in the kitchen.[4]
- Hardly any house in India is equipped with fire alarms; moreover, most electrical hardware stores do not even carry one. When I asked them why, they said fires are not a major hazard in India. Strangely enough, during 2006 I personally experienced two incidents of fires in the same house, starting from electrical circuits.
- It takes about three minutes for a small fire to erupt into a flashover. That is, when a room grows so hot suddenly everything bursts into flames.

Despite all this, only one in four Americans has devised and practiced a plan for escaping from home during a fire.[3] Furthermore, when smoke alarms went off, only 8% thought there was a fire and should get out.[3]

Does this mean that by and large, we (the human element) cannot prevent disasters even from known causes? Is it the way we think and operate that sows the seeds for such events, or do we live in our worlds with blissful ignorance? Yet, when such things happen, we choose to label them as accidents. Do we call them accidents out of convenience or to save face? Regardless, what paradigms are we creating for the future? More importantly, does this type of thinking and behavior carry over into other facets of life?

While writing this book, I looked for parallels between such observations from personal life and the business world. That journey uncovered a stark similarity. It is well known that a majority of businesses do not work out in the long term, and few mergers and acquisitions succeed.[5] The lifetimes of most businesses mimic that of the owner, as seen from these examples: RK films from India, Woolworth stores in the U.S., and Austin Motor Company in the U.K. These are three of many I can cite from personal observations across the world, from developing and developed countries.

Each company rose to fame with the founder. After the founder passed away, the company either extinguished quickly or went into decay, eventually closing its doors or getting absorbed and losing its identity and status. Apple Computer in the U.S., and Kirloskar in India have shown similar symptoms (based on studying what happened when the founders were not at the helm). Time will tell if they will rise above this cycle or become part of it. Of course, there are exceptions such as: Siemens, Larsen and Toubro, Toyota, and Frito Lay. However, they are in the minority, and in such cases, the mindset behind the operation and execution of the business is rather different. Intel seems to be on a similar path after suffering at the hands of Japanese competitors during the early 1980s.

Then there is the breakup of Daimler Chrysler. The two united in 1998, the largest industrial merger to date. They intended to create a global enterprise with presence in every major world market and to offer products to all segments of the markets they served. Their union lasted less than 10 years.

We can also cite scores of other examples where businesses simply cease to exist for other reasons. Statistics indicate most new businesses will ultimately fail.[5] According to Hart Posen, Assistant Professor of Strategy at the Ross Business School, University of Michigan, more than 80 percent of businesses fail, and 10 percent of all American companies fold each year.[5] This means business success is a rarity rather than the norm.

Deborah Barrie, a Business Development Coach, gives 13 common causes of business failure:[6,7]

1. Poor cash flow management.
2. Absence of performance monitoring.
3. Lack of understanding or use of performance monitoring Information.
4. Poor debtor management.
5. Over borrowing. The company is over leveraged and debt is not being reduced.
6. Over-reliance on a few key customers.
7. Poor market research leading to an inaccurate understanding of the target customer's wants and needs.
8. Lack of financial skills and planning.
9. Failure to innovate.
10. Poor inventory management.
11. Poor communications throughout the organization.
12. Failure to recognize your own strengths and weaknesses.
13. Trying to go it alone.

There are similar listings on the Internet, in business books such as *Built to Last* by Collins and Porras, and *The E Myth Revisited* by Michael Gerber. In each of the 13 causes of business failures, we find the human element as a contributing factor, just as in the house burning down, however, when a business fails, no one calls it an accident.

What is amiss with the human element? Was Andrew Grove the Co-founder and CEO of Intel right when he wrote *Only the Paranoid Survive?* Do we need to re-visit our ability to define, understand, and manage risk? What could be better than learning from our own mistakes in Risk Management? Join me in the journey. As a species, we have a long way to go. Indeed, if you can prevent just one disaster from the information in this book, I will feel rewarded, and it will give clear testimony to the learning capabilities of the human race. Let us start now with a look at some of the notable events of the last three decades as mentioned in Chapter 1.

Sources:
1. http://www.usfa.dhs.gov/downloads/pdf/tfrs/v4i4.pdf
2. http://www.southwales-fire.gov.uk/SWFSCMS/OurPerformance /statistics.htm
3. http://ci.marshfield.wi.us/fd/firestats.htm
4. http://www.nrma.com.au/pub/nrma/home/homehelp/secure-protect/housefires/index.shtml
5. http://www.ns.umich.edu/htdocs/releases/story .php?id=478
6. http://www.canadabusiness.ca/alberta/newsletter/May2003.html
7. http://www.cbsc.org/servlet/ContentServer?cid=1104766631924 &pagename=CBSC_AB%2FCBSC_WebPage%2FCBSC_WebPageTemp& c=CBSC_WebPage

Part I

Did These Have To Happen?

Chapter 1

Accidents, Acts of Nature, or...?

Risks...We all take them.
Mistakes...We all make them.
And then...Lay Blame.

Consider the following events:

1979 – The Three Mile Island incident
   A serious accident at a nuclear power plant in the U.S.

1984 – The Bhopal tragedy
   Several thousands died when poisonous methyl–isocynate gas
   leaked from a Union Carbide plant in India.

1986 – Space Shuttle Challenger is lost
   All aboard, perish. Some cite the O-rings, others claim faulty
   decision-making as the culprit, and yet others point to lack of
   proper statistical analysis.

1986 – Chernobyl Power Plant disaster in Russia
   Thousands feel the effects in the way of health and
   environmental problems.

1990 – Hyundai cars have defective hood latches
    Hoods can potentially fly open on Hyundai Sonatas in the U.S.

1996 – Value Jet plane is lost in Florida everglades
    No survivors. Investigation showed it was due to improperly
    stored oxygen generators in the cargo hold.

1998 – Woolworth closes last stores in the U.S.
    A one-time retail giant ceases to exist.

1999 – GE appliance has potential for a switch to melt and ignite
    Recall issued for 3.1 million dishwashers.

2001 – The 9/11 Tragedy
    Thousands of lives lost as terrorists strike at the World Trade
    Center and the Pentagon in the U.S.

2001 – Enron, a major U.S. based oil company collapses
    The company was declared a powerhouse less than a year
    before. Thousands lose their life's savings.

2002 – WorldCom collapses
    A major telecommunications company in the U.S. faces
    financial disaster.

2003 – Columbia disintegrates on re-entry
    All astronauts on board perish. Debris scattered over vast parts
    of the U.S.

2004 – Tsunami of Biblical proportions
    An earthquake causes the tsunami that hits Indonesia, and
    other Asian countries, hundreds of thousands lives are lost.

2005 – London hit by terror strikes
Terrorists leave Britons badly shaken.

2005 – Hurricane Katrina hits New Orleans
The city suffers wholesale destruction. The death toll is
estimated in the thousands.

2005 – Earthquake in Pakistan and India
Tens of thousands perish. Weeks after the tragic incident,
relief and aid slowly arrive.

2006 – Sago Mine disaster in West Virginia, U.S.
Over a dozen miners trapped, many believe this did not have
to happen. The life saving apparatus was found to be
dysfunctional.

2006 – Comair plane crash in the U.S.
The plane, assigned to the wrong runway, crashes during
takeoff at Lexington, Kentucky. Fifty lives are lost.

It is too late when possibilities turn into failures.

Now, answer the following questions:

- Which of these can be considered acts of nature?
- Which of these were foreseeable?
- Which ones were preventable?
- Can we label any of these as accidents?
- *Should* we label any of these as accidents?
- Could the risk from any of these be determined beforehand?
- What is the tangible cost, and the intangible cost?

Chapter 2

What Would You Do?
A Self-Assessment

Answer the following questions, without putting in any extra effort above and beyond the usual way you work or think. For those that involve math, please don't make any calculations. Just select the answers from the choices provided based on your best judgment.

Question #1:

You have driven home on the same road every day and usually experience a smooth ride. Today, however, you notice a considerable amount of loose debris on the road as though a gravel truck had passed through ahead of you. You pass farms on either side and notice the flowers and vineyards in full bloom. You've always enjoyed this scenery after a hard day at work. You see a truck approaching somewhat fast but nothing out of the ordinary. All of a sudden, you see bushes to your right quiver. A small rabbit darts across the road.

Your knee-jerk reaction would be to:
   a. Hit the brakes.
   b. Swerve to avoid the rabbit.
   c. Just drive on.

Question #2:

Select the best answer by estimating the value for e^4.

a. 0.09

b. 59

NOTE: e = 2.718

Question #3:

Suppose you have successfully managed a growing company for the last seven years. You and your team have developed several proprietary products and have a treasure of specialties and business secrets that served your business well. Now someone has alerted you that one of your employees plans to strike out on his own with a similar business just a few hundred yards down the road. Based on your observations and interactions with the employee, you have never had any reason to suspect his behavior or intentions.

Which of these will you most likely do?

a. Fire him immediately without giving any reason.

b. Transfer him to a department where he cannot gain any more knowledge or sensitive information about your business.

c. Hire a private investigator to learn more about his motives and intentions.

Question #4:

The product of $1 \times 1 \times 2 \times 2 \times 3 \times 3 \times 4 \times 4 \times 5 \times 5$ is which of the following? Without using a calculator, select the best answer from the following:

a. 125

b. 2500

c. Over 10,000

Question #5:
You are leading a project that is currently on schedule and expect to finish it on time. One of the activities requires you to obtain the city's permission (critical to the survival of the company) beforehand, but this will mean a delay of over a month. In the past, with a history of more than 100 projects, you had always started this type of activity before obtaining such permission, and it has never been an issue.

In this case, you will:
a. Go ahead with the activity and worry about getting permission later, using the past performance as a rationale for your decision.
b. Ensure the permission is obtained first, regardless of the time pressures.
c. Ask to be relieved of this project and given some other assignment.

Question #6:
Read a, b, and c, then answer d quickly:
a. The Statue of Liberty is in the State of New York.
b. Wine bottles are usually closed with a cork.
c. One of the cutlery items used to eat food with is called fork.
d. Meat that pigs eat is called _____.

Question #7:
Which statement appeals to you the most?
a. I'll believe it when I see it.
b. I'll see it when I believe it.
c. I'll believe it when I can feel it.
d. I'll feel it when I believe it.

Question #8:

Select the most accurate answer based on what you know at this moment about the space shuttle program. Do not research the answer.

a. The Challenger was lost due to an O-ring problem.

b. The Columbia was lost due to an O-ring problem.

c. The Challenger is still flying.

Question #9:

Which of the following is the number two car manufacturer in the world? Do not research for the answer.

a. Toyota

b. Ford

c. GM

d. Chrysler

e. Honda

Question #10:

Without using a calculator, your best estimate for the product of $400 \times 36 \times 1$ is:

a. Over 9,999

b. 500

c. 125

Question #11:

Which will cause more severe burns: boiling water, or water at $212^\circ F$?

Question #12:

Two days after the day before the day before yesterday is Saturday. What day is today?

a. Thursday
b. Friday
c. Saturday
d. Sunday
e. None of the above

Question #13:

From the following, identify which would be failure mode(s) for a pager or a cell phone.

a. Dead battery
b. Out of range
c. Unclear or unreadable display

Question #14:

You happen to be traveling in India and see the Swastika displayed prominently in one of the call centers your company uses. You conclude:

a. Someone related to the Nazis put up the sign to scare you.
b. The call center is run by people affiliated with Nazis.
c. It is a symbol of good luck and well-being.

Question #15:

Without using a calculator, your best estimate for the product of 72 × 400 is:

a. 125
b. 2500
c. Over 10,000

Part II

Mistakes We Make

Chapter 3

Is Anything Risk Free?

The human species seems to be losing its ability to prevent failures. While technology can and will help, it is a double-edged sword. Throughout this book, you will learn more on why we do the things we do, and gain knowledge of invaluable tools and techniques that you can use. All this is focused on increasing your ability to manage risk and get ahead of the curve. Nothing can create a *Risk Free* state; therefore, aiming to achieve that is pointless.

Risk is unavoidable No risk—no reward; no pain—no gain. I know you've heard this before; perhaps even used it to justify your decisions every now and then. Like most aphorisms, the general applicability of this statement has its limits. We must, and do take risks, sometimes prudently and sometimes recklessly, although we may not acknowledge the latter. Reckless risks offer a sure invitation to failure, therefore, we need to become astute in taking prudent risks.

As you read this section, you may think it is easy to see an action or decision as a reckless risk or mistake in hindsight. After all, no one could possibly recognize it as reckless when it was happening. Think again. I see at least two problems with such thinking.

First, *it is possible* to identify many of these mistakes before they occur and sidestep them, but too often, we don't. Then, instead of recognizing the error, we tend to justify our actions.

Second, hindsight does not offer as clear a view as we think because hindsight relies so much on memory, which is very subjective and malleable. We have an uncanny ability to engage in selective recall. Hence, we cannot always provide an accurate description of the past, more so if there is high emotion attached to such recall.

Think about each of the disasters pointed out in Chapter 1 *Accidents, Acts of Nature, or...* Were they truly accidents? Except for tsunamis and earthquakes, they were all preventable. If you accept that premise, then you must wonder why they were not prevented? How can rational individuals let such things happen? If we don't take the time to study and discover the causes, we'll continue to depend on chance instead of sensible choice.

As we discuss the *Ten Mistakes* that lead to unnecessary risks, I encourage you to look for parallels you have seen in your life, in businesses, in governments, in non-profit organizations, in public, and private companies. It will help to bear in mind that these ten are not the only ones; rather, they represent some of the most common errors. Each of these *Ten Mistakes* can precipitate failure and/or cause high risk. The mistakes may occur individually or in combination with others. Further, you will also realize that one mistake can lead to another.

Although I will present and discuss each on a standalone basis, you may find them occurring in groups or in certain sequences. The exact sequence in which they might occur is rather hard to predict. For example, in one case you may find that the Trap of Comfort Zone develops after a mix up between Signal and Noise. In another case, you may find the opposite is true.

I will discuss how to avoid these mistakes separately, and I encourage you not to jump to that chapter before understanding all Ten Mistakes. Taking a shortcut will shortchange your ability to prevent these mistakes.

Working through the exercises in different parts of the book will help increase your awareness and skill at spotting each mistake as it occurs, rather than after the fact.

Now, let us get started with looking at each of the *Ten Mistakes*. They are as follows:

1   The Terribility Factor
2   Recency and Frequency
3   The Illusion of Control
4   The Trap of Comfort Zones
5   No Time for Risk Analysis
6   Confidence Without Competence
7   Ignoring the Time and Space Dimensions
8   The Tip of the Iceberg
9   Mixing up Signal and Noise
10   Rationalization

Chapter 4

Mistake 1
The Terribility Factor

Terribility is that which creates extreme emotion due to the severity of an incident. As a result, it turns off rational thinking, which causes us to *overreact and overcompensate*. We will look at how this affects our actions and decisions, and culminates in mistakes that lead to poor risk management.

To begin with, let us examine the responses when I asked dozens of people what they thought about the idea of using nuclear power. They said they didn't like it, and gave a variety of reasons.

"It's dangerous."

"It's risky."

"Damage from a nuclear accident lasts a long time and can cause widespread death and destruction."

"Storage of nuclear waste is a problem."

Most people associate a mushroom cloud with nuclear power, a terrifying image. It is repulsive, isn't it? You are not alone. However, should we generalize such images?

At the time of this writing in 2006, the world braces itself for yet another energy shortage. Wildly fluctuating gas prices have been in an upward trend, and India and China now use more oil than ever before.[2] During the time of low oil prices, a few years ago, auto manufacturers in the U.S. ramped up production of Sport Utility Vehicles (SUVs) and large pickup trucks while offering little improvement in gas mileage. In one of his speeches, President George W. Bush commented, "We are addicted to oil."

Rolling blackouts, a routine occurrence in the Third World, now looms on the horizon for the U.S. Iran threatens to create situations where oil prices could rise beyond $100 per barrel[3], yet, every time someone suggests the use of nuclear power as a possible solution, people cringe.

Then, I presented the same people with the following facts/reports:

* ❖ In 2005, about 43,000 people perished in automobile accidents in the U.S. alone, and worldwide, that number might easily exceed 100,000.[4] This is by far in excess of the harm ever caused by any nuclear accident to date, and so many lives are lost *every year* in automobile accidents.

* ❖ In the U.S., an estimated 195,000 people die *each year* from medical mistakes.[5]

* ❖ About 40,000 children under the age of five die *each day* from malnutrition and preventable diseases worldwide.[1]

So, I asked, how do these stack up against the track record of nuclear power? They expressed disbelief at these facts.

Differing perceptions of risk While nuclear power has its opponents, it also has supporters. For example, France gets 80 percent of its power from nuclear sources while the U.S. and Japan get 19 and 29 percent respectively. All three countries are among the top 10 nuclear power producing countries, and each has a high

Gross Domestic Product. Do U.S. and Japan look at it with more dread than France? Why? Could we attribute it to the negativism produced by the use of nuclear weapons? Perhaps. *Is the Terribility factor at work here?*

In 1979 after the Three Mile Island accident in the U.S., the Swedish parliament decided not to build any more nuclear power plants and to phase out existing plants by 2010. The Chernobyl accident reinforced that thinking in the 1990s, and the Swedes started cutting back on the use of nuclear power.[6] Recently, concerns over staying competitive have reversed their opinion, and Sweden has ramped up energy production from nuclear power. In addition, existing power plants will likely stay in operation until 2050. Other countries are also experiencing a similar reversal of opinion, that is, until another event hijacks rational thought.

Emotions and reactions Neither the corporate world nor the government can claim immunity from irrational thought because of the *Terribility Factor*. When extreme emotions rise beyond a certain point, rational thought flies out the window. Scandals revolving around behaviors of high-ranking officials have happened in the past and continue to transpire. It seems the tightening of legal requirements occurs only after bad behaviors hit a nerve and lawmakers hurry to put controls in place, which should have been there anyway. Over the last two decades we've seen knee-jerk reactions taking the form of controls such as the Sarbanes Oxley Act, FDA's reporting requirements with regard to drugs and medical devices, California's ruling on the use of cell phones while driving, and laws related to the prevention of terrorism. Some of this we now realize is overreaction as we see companies shying away from raising capital and getting listed on the U.S. Stock Markets, and, governments relaxing their over bearing controls which were installed in the after math of terrorist attacks.

The toll of such behavior results in focusing on certain aspects while other serious social and business issues are ignored. This can carry on for years. Here are three of many.

- People from certain communities will risk dying of thirst rather than accept water from a person of a supposedly *lower* community in the belief that doing so will contaminate them. This continues to alienate hundreds of thousands in several countries, despite laws that make such discrimination illegal.

- Blinded by competitive pressures and the need to demonstrate profitability quarter to quarter, many companies in the U.S. outsource without adequate assessment of supplier capabilities. Meanwhile, the Germans (Mercedes Benz), Japanese (Toyota), and Koreans (Samsung) build new factories and plants in the U.S.

- Trying to escape the pain of losing an election, politicians overrule the law of the land to appease minorities. The myopic action of vote gathering trumps the long-term interests of the nation.

The Terribility Factor rivets your attention, and hijacks rational thinking!
What was your answer to question 11 in Chapter 2?

Sources:
1. http://www.rehydrate.org/facts/ten_facts.htm
2. http://www.state.gov/e/eeb/rls/rm/2005/66574.htm
3. http://www.fromthewilderness.com/free/ww3/011806_world_stories.shtml
4. http://blogs.usatoday.com/ondeadline/2006/08/highway_fatalit.htm
5. http://www.eweek.com/article2/0,1895,1628348,00.asp
6. http://www.uic.com.au/nip39.htm

Chapter 5

Mistake 2
Recency and Frequency

Recent events are usually the easiest to recall, and, when something happens with increasing frequency, whether good or bad, we tend to get carried away by it. *Recency and Frequency* acting together or individually can thus overcome rationality.

Frequent and recent events loom large From June to December of 1973 I worked as an in-plant trainee at a large electrical equipment manufacturer near Bombay, India as part of my degree program. One day in July, I arrived late for work, and the training manager called me into his office.

"You don't understand the implications of coming in late frequently," thundered Mr. Chandrachud. "The plant's attendance policy indicates that anyone arriving more than five minutes past reporting time is considered late. We can cancel your in-plant training program for such tardiness."

I had never imagined not graduating in 1974 over something as silly as this. For me, getting to the plant included a 15-minute walk, a 65-minute train ride, and a 20-minute bus ride. The time clock at the entrance was an old mechanical punch clock, known for its inaccuracy. I am sure it had an elastic pendulum. In addition, during monsoon season, trains ran late. The 80-inch downpour over three months frequently flooded the tracks and I

31

had to deal with all of this every day. Of course, none of this mattered to my boss. I wondered why he picked on me when others also arrived late. My delays caused no disruption, nor did they create any safety issues, so what was the fuss about?

Two months later, the first shift employees staged a walkout because of Mr. Chandrachud's nagging over relatively minor issues beyond their control. For them, the cumulative psychological stress had reached a snapping point. When minor issues add up over time, the mind eventually equates them with the same level of pain as a severe one-time incident. A strong, knee-jerk reaction quickly follows without regard for consequences. This walkout resulted in several weeks of late shipments and loss of orders from irate clients. Luckily, the second shift employees were spared Mr. Chandrachud's ire because he worked the day shift, and the second shift reported for work just as he left.

The fixation on occurrence can mislead in two ways. In the above case, we saw the effects of a high rate of occurrence. In other cases, however, it can be rather low, creating a false sense of confidence that an event will not happen.

Consider the space shuttle Columbia. NASA had flown more than 100 missions, and on every one of them, insulating foam had come off, however, it had never resulted in a safety issue.[1] No missions were compromised despite the possibility of foam debris striking the shuttle in sensitive areas. When Flight Readiness Review for the Columbia took place on January 9, 2003, the mission management team concluded that the effects of debris did not pose a concern for the safety of the Columbia.[2] It was launched successfully, but the mission ended in a tragedy.

Recency and Frequency are over bearing, thus both mislead!
What was your answer to question 6 in Chapter 2?

Sources:
1.   http://www.floridatoday.com/columbia/columbiastory 2A48513A.htm
2.   http://www.nasa.gov/columbia/foia/index.html

Chapter 6

Mistake 3
The Illusion of Control

The illusion of control leads us to believe we have control over the outcomes, when in reality we may not. It is a dangerous phenomenon, and it can occur in dealing with equipment, people, organizations, or any operation. The illusion of control causes us to take charge of things when we may have been better off otherwise. Yet, when flying, we place our lives in the hands of pilots, and automated control systems of the airplane without hesitation.

Three years ago, I interviewed a senior manager, a Mr. W, from a Fortune 500 company to discuss Risk Management. His company designs and manufactures complex equipment and has a global presence with annual sales exceeding $8 billion in 2003. He had joined the company six years before and had over ten years of previous engineering and management experience.

As we discussed the topic of risk, he made a casual comment. "Anything can happen. I could get struck by lightning while walking to my car in the parking lot. I can't do anything about it. If lightning has to strike, it will. I still have to walk to the car. I've done it many times in the past and nothing has ever happened to me. But you know, there's a trick to it." He continued to share what he perceived was the secret to not getting struck by lightning.

I had heard such comments before, so I presented him with this scenario.

Suppose while flying on a business trip, the plane begins to shake, and the pilot announces, "We're running into severe weather. I can circle around the clouds for a while, but that will delay our arrival by over 30 minutes. So, I've decided to take a chance and fly through the bad weather. I hope you'll understand."

Mr. W gave me a wide-eyed look. I just smiled and asked, "So, what do you think of the pilot's decision?"

Without hesitation he said, "He shouldn't be taking chances with other people's lives."

This response, typical of what I've heard in other interviews, poses some disturbing questions. Why do we consider risk acceptable if we undertake it of our own accord and for ourselves, but not okay if someone else subjects us to it?

Often times we think we can control situations and outcomes because we are familiar with them. This sets the stage for undertaking "Reckless Risks" such as rowing against the stream

> **The Illusion of Control**
>
> *In a study of the illusion of control in a population of traders working in investment banks, Fenton-O'Creevy et al (2003-2004) found that traders who were prone to high illusion of control had significantly worse performance on analysis, risk management, and contribution to desk profits. They also earned significantly less.*
> (Source:
> http://en.wikipedia.org/wiki/ Illusion_ of_ control.)

34

atop Niagara Falls. At other times, the basis for such confidence lies in something we've seen, or heard. When chance occurrences lead to successful or expected outcomes, they reinforce the mistaken belief that we are in control.

Mr. W ended our interview with this comment. "The trick is to walk next to trees and poles. Nothing, nothing has ever happened to me."

I didn't argue with him. He wasn't ready to listen yet.

We experience similar phenomena in our daily lives as well, for example, when we sit in the front passenger's seat, and allow someone else to drive. This loss of control makes us nervous, even if the driver is *more careful* behind the wheel than us. Let us look at situations where humans, machines, and systems interact.

If you drive fast enough on a wet road, your car will aquaplane, a phenomenon that occurs when tires lose contact with the ground and begin riding on a thin film of water. You will notice it easier in cars without power steering than those with, because all of a sudden the steering feels easier to turn. You must pay attention to notice this, however.

In a car with power steering, you would continue to believe you remain in control, and realize the problem only when the car fails to steer as needed.

In this simple system that includes the elements of driver, road, car, and rain, one can easily see how things work. In case of complex machines or systems, such visibility is lacking. Often built-in mechanisms to maintain control hide real problems, since they can force the overall system to function normally via compensation.

When Columbia re-entered the earth's atmosphere, increasing drag on the left wing due to damage from the debris would have caused a change in trajectory. However, the onboard computers, control, and feedback systems intervened, making sure the shuttle's nose pointed in the right direction.[1]

The Role and Nature of Feedback in Systems

There are two types of systems: Open Loop, and Closed Loop. The Open Loop system uses pre-set models or programs, compares the current state of the system to the program, and drives the system accordingly. In this case, a feedback loop based on actual performance does not exist as shown in Figure 1. A simple example is that of a fan; based on the setting high, medium, or low, the fan speed is governed but the actual speed is not monitored by the system itself. Closed Loop systems monitor the output to create feedback as shown in Figure 2. In the aquaplaning example, the feel of the steering and the direction of the car, serve as feedbacks for the driver. The control is not automatic, but it is manual and exercised by the driver.

Open Loop System Since an Open Loop system operates based on a setting, once it is pre-set, it may give the impression of being in control. Thus, it can easily mislead. In one case, a company used spending on new product development as a key business metric. They measured the spending and thought everything was fine.

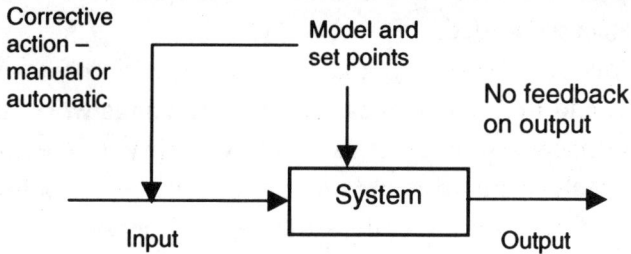

Corrective action – manual or automatic

Model and set points

No feedback on output

System

Input

Output

Figure 1. Open Loop System

For some time the company did very well, but 3 quarters later, changing market conditions caused a severe decline in performance. Management, used to measure the spending levels, continued to believe it was doing the right thing.In reality, the

36

products it had in development no longer appealed to customers. Because of the very nature of Open Loop systems, the company lacked a feedback loop and was blindsided by a competitor.

Closed Loop System   Unlike an open loop system, a closed loop system uses feedback to track the gap between output and the set point. Based on this gap, system performance is adjusted. The adjustment may be done manually or automatically.

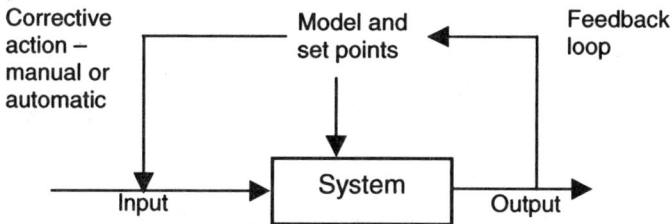

Figure 2. Closed Loop System

In this case, the illusion of control can set in when the feedback loop's function is impaired, interrupted, misunderstood, or when the system can automatically correct itself, which makes system performance appear as normal regardless of the true state of the system. Several factors affect the performance of systems such as inertia, damping characteristics, and the rate of change from one stage to another. Each creates the potential for making mistakes and risks. Consider these examples.

Earlier we saw how the trajectory of the Columbia was maintained despite drag from the left wing, which was due to irregular surfaces at the leading edge. It was a system with automatic control systems.[1] Similar problems can be encountered with systems that have manual controls as well. The Chernobyl power plant experienced problems while under manual control.

When powering down the reactor to conduct an experiment aimed at improving safety of the system, the operator shut off the automatic controls. He did not make allowances for the reactor's self-damping behavior, so the reactor slowed down to 1% of capacity instead of the targeted 25%. Operation in such low ranges is unstable, and irregularities in nuclear fission result. Coupled with other mistakes, this error culminated in the explosions that blew the roof off the reactor. For a more detailed analysis of the situation please read pages 28-35 in *The Logic of Failure* by Dietrich Dorner.

We can find everyday examples in our lives. Let's look at a fever, a symptom of a brewing medical condition. We can choose to suppress it with over-the-counter medication, creating the illusion of control. This can actually make conditions worse if the body is unable to fight off the infection. The same holds true for itching, rashes, coughs, runny noses, and other such ailments. In each case, the question we have to ask is are we suppressing the symptoms to create the illusion of control? Is it control or is it deception?

Illusion of Control: Maintaining course gives no assurance you will reach the destination!
What did you answer to question 1 in Chapter 2?

Sources:
1. http://www.io.com/~o_m/clfaq/old/columbia_loss_faq_s5.html#Best_guess

Chapter 7

Mistake 4
The Trap of Comfort Zones

Have you ever seen a freely suspended drop of water in the form of a cube? Why does it tend to become spherical? Nature has it that a sphere puts the water drop in a state of minimum energy, the comfort zone for the water drop. However, it lasts only as long as no other force or object acts upon it. Left alone, the water drop has control over what shape it will take, based on the built-in (natural) molecular forces. Therefore, it becomes spherical automatically. Neither science, nor humans created it that way; we just discovered the phenomena. Let us study the consequences of our comfort zones.

According to *Investors Business Daily*, one of the top ten mistakes people make in investing is buying stocks that pay a dividend. The payment is automatic, and the comfort comes from seeing a dividend check (Remember those days when you regularly got a paycheck?) in the mailbox periodically. It is predictable and arrives every quarter. "Dividends may seem like defensive armor in a bad market, but sharp capital losses can pierce that armor," says David Saito-Chung.[1]

Another mistake in the top ten for investing is that people don't cut their losses quickly enough. Instead, they hold on to a losing stock in the hope that it will turn around. They also have the added pain in admitting they made a wrong decision. Consequently they find excuses and take comfort in staying put, hoping it will come back. They fail to realize that a swift corrective action, while painful in the short run, can lead to much better results down the road. As they hold on, people rationalize their actions by saying, "I'm a long-term investor." In fact, the market has a mind of its own, and it doesn't care whether they are a long term or short-term investor, neither does it care what they think or how they feel.

Habits Aristotle said, "Men acquire a particular quality by constantly acting in a particular way...you become just by performing just actions, temperate by performing temperate actions, brave by performing brave actions." In much the same way, my elders taught me, "First we define our habits, then they define us." Once we define our habits and behavior and act accordingly on a regular basis, we begin to act automatically, and operate in our *comfort zone.*

Psychologists have recognized this automatic processing and response for a very long time.[2] It developed as a vital part of our existence, yet it turns into a severe handicap when we must do things that require conscious effort. Balancing a bicycle offers a good example. We wobble a great deal as a learner, but with practice, we can multi-task as we ride along. Driving is analogous.

An action or skill is considered automatic when it meets three conditions:

1. It occurs without intent.
2. It does not give rise to conscious awareness.
3. It does not interfere with other mental activities.

These three together create a hideous comfort trap. It is so effective that it can make people totally blind to critical matters. An Indian folktale gives us a great example. As the story goes, two Indian princes sat comfortably engrossed in their game of chess to the point of oblivion; meanwhile they ignored giving timely directions to their army commander in the throes of war. You can guess the outcome.

Such mental conditioning can happen for several reasons, so we must stay vigilant. One woman I know has an extreme "I" dimension (Introverted, as described by the Myers Briggs Profile). She prefers to avoid dealing with people. She does not have a job and keeps postponing or finding excuses to stay away from applying for one. Her attempts at running a small business have resulted in nothing but failures. Despite all this, she refuses to accept the facts, face her reality, and do something about it. Instead, she depends on social security payments to survive. The grip of her comfort zone is just too tight.

Habits of organizations The comfort trap afflicts organizations as well. Take this case of a group of middle and upper level business managers. Once a week they would meet to discuss the state of projects and project teams within the company. The managers talked about the performance of the project teams, which department needed to take action on what, and once a month, they discussed budgetary matters for the company. The weekly meeting had become such a ritual that, regardless of how badly the company needed the managers out in the field talking to customers or visiting suppliers, they would not miss this meeting.

Yes, they regularly received information from the field; however, it came filtered through two layers. They heard what they wanted to hear, in turn reinforcing their comfort zone.

In another situation during 2004, the VP of one of the banks we do business with came to see me at my office. He said it was a courtesy visit, and we talked for nearly an hour. He explained, "The bank has asked us to make regular visits to its clients to better understand how the bank was serving them."

I suspect this came after Bank of America launched customer service improvement initiatives where the bank staff started developing more of a personal relationship with their clients.

41

After the usual exchange of pleasantries, he asked me, "How is our bank taking care of you? Would you like for us to do anything differently?"

I looked at him skeptically. "Do you *really* want to know?"

"Yes, of course," he answered.

I then shared what our staff had recently experienced.

"I waited in line for more than 18 minutes for a teller, and it is not unusual for this to occur."

"The teller needed to get a higher level signature for deposits, and I had to wait again."

"The bank charged a $5 fee for travelers checks and refused to waive these charges even for long time loyal customers."

I went on to cite Bank of America and Bank One's services. I had definitely jolted his comfort zone, and he began to ramble on about the merits of their tellers, their error-free record, and so forth, typical of what average managers would do when they hear things that put them outside of their comfort zone.

"Error free record? That's a given." I said. "How can you claim credit for something that's as basic as being accurate in transactions?"

Needless to say, the VP barely spoke with me after that day, and at the time of this writing, in December 2006, the bank continues with their old behaviors. Why? Because that is their comfort zone. Meanwhile, we have switched banks. Thanks to free markets, there are plenty of choices.

Comfort zones work like gold plated shackles. You get enslaved despite knowing they limit you.
What was your answer to question 5 in Chapter 2?

Sources:
1. http://www.investors.com/yahoofinance/ 2004w42/storya05.asp
2. Stephen Reed, *Cognition Theory and Applications,* 2004, 58

Chapter 8

Mistake 5
No Time for Risk Analysis

We don't seem to have enough time, and it is becoming a universal feeling across individuals, companies, governments, and nations. We often use the excuse of *No Time for Risk Analysis* to avoid due diligence and to skip simple, yet sound precautions against reckless risks.

Ironically, the day still takes 24 hours as always, and there still are 365 days in the year. The pace of time remains the same, then, why do we feel a shortage of time? What has changed? Time is an equal opportunity phenomenon. Each of us *has* the same number of hours in the day! Could it be that this feeling has more to do with who and what we are?

Pace of time and personality During my work with a leading medical products manufacturing firm in the 1980s, I had the opportunity to observe two marketing managers closely. One, I will call him JV, often did extensive research, surveys, and analysis before putting together a forecast for the following year. I call this *Ready—Aim—Fire*. The other manager felt rushed all the time, and operated mostly by hunches based on previous years' performances, *Ready—Fire—Aim*, with minimal data analysis. This was not a one-time occurrence but happened repeatedly over several years. One behaved as though constantly short of time, while the other operated in a calm and controlled manner.

Having observed such behavior in different organizations, and settings, I wondered if there was an innate preference to act and behave one way over the other? If so, how could we determine who has what preference? Since this had to do with behavior, it depended on three key factors: circumstances, attitudes, and personalities. Of these, the last two are people related, and therefore they can be understood via personality analysis.

The personality of an individual is the integration of past experiences and what nature gave us, in short, Nature and Nurture. The research took me to Dr. Richard Grant, a practicing psychologist and counselor from Austin, Texas.

Dr. Grant uses the Myers Briggs Type Indicator® (MBTI) to study personality. Its roots lie in the works of Dr. Carl Jung, the famous Swiss psychologist from the early 1900s. Myers and Briggs expanded upon Jung's work, and the model bears their names. According to Myers and Briggs, we can study human personality using four dimensions. Each dimension deals with a particular aspect of human preferences. These are:

1. Introversion or Extraversion (I or E)
2. Sensing or iNtuiting (S or N)
3. Feeling or Thinking (F or T)
4. Judging or Perceiving (J or P)

While I'd love to elaborate on each, we will discuss only those more relevant to how we think, make decisions, and take action. Therefore, we will therefore discuss three dimensions: Sensing or iNtuiting, Feeling or Thinking, and Judging or Perceiving.

Sensing or iNtuiting   Sensing means paying attention to what is going on outside, whereas iNtuiting means listening to the internal voice. Another way of looking at this is observation or introspection. It isn't that we do one or the other exclusively, but more importantly, which do we do more often, and which one do we prefer.

Feeling or Thinking   We must ask ourselves, "Do I tend to focus more on feelings or thoughts?" The former follows the heart, and more gets done based on emotion and desire. The latter works more by reasoning. Thinkers are considered tough minded and sometimes heartless.

Judging or Perceiving   These preferences deal with whether a person judiciously makes and keeps schedules and agendas or probes and keeps options open to avoid getting tied down. Probers want to keep their eyes open for chances to do things they want while schedulers tend to stop looking and drive things to closure. The two can drive each other nuts!

I discussed my observations of the two marketing managers and other similar situations concerning risks and decision making with Dr. Richard Grant. He suggested it was due to the J/P preference in human personality. For the Js of the world, the driving motivation is evaluation, implicit judgment followed by gathering information, and driving to closure. The Ps prefer to explore, and take joy in the immediacy of events and actions. They view analysis, structure, and rules as temporary, meant only to exploit the opportunity.

The implicit judgment of the Js and their tendency to operate in the countdown mode can result in the *No Time for Risk Analysis* syndrome. Consequently, they may overlook the sources of risk. Once they are convinced that risk analysis is the right thing to do, they will most likely work through the mechanics with diligence.

The openness of the P, on the other hand, can prove valuable in dealing with the "What ifs." Thus, the best way to do risk analysis is to have a balance of the J and P preference in the team. The J will see the tip of the iceberg and chart the course based on operating rules. The P will be more open to look below the waterline to identify what else is out there.

DISC – A Four Dimensional Model

Another method to study behavior is the DISC approach, based on the theories of Harvard Psychologist William Moulton Marston.[1] He developed the DISC model and wrote about it in his 1928 book, *Emotions of Normal People*. Over the years, several others have revised and expanded on his ideas.

According to this model, we can think of human behavior in terms of four dimensions: Drive or Determination (Dominance), Influence (Sociability), Steadfastness (Thoughtfulness), and Conscientiousness (Compliance). Each deserves some further explanation. We need to remember that every behavioral style has its strengths and weaknesses.

General Traits Within Each Dimension

D: Controlling, assertive, and arrogant; high D's are very demanding, forceful, and strong-willed, whereas as low D's are conservative, calculating, cautious, agreeable, and peaceful. A high D may potentially be more prone to feel rushed and short of time.

I: Optimistic, convincing, and persuasive; they have the ability to function within society and communicate with others. High I's are likely talkative and do things to influence others. Low I's are not persuaded with feelings but rather with data and facts.

S: Tenacious, patient, thoughtful, deliberate, and diplomatic; they may work in the background. High S's are known to be good listeners and careful with change. Low S's tend toward impatience and impulsiveness.

C: Structured, organized, and conscientious; high C's are thoughtful planners. Detail oriented, they take responsibility very seriously, focus on quality, are passive, and controlled. Low C's tend to break or test rules and are casual or careless in their approach. They can become obstinate and hard to work with.

I present DISC and the Myers Briggs Type Indicator systems because both are widely used for understanding people's preferences and behaviors. At some point, you might encounter these, if you haven't already. In the chapter on Antidotes you will see how this knowledge can be used for better risk management. Some people have a built-in preference to operate in the *No Time for Risk Analysis* mode. It is like a disease, and you will need to guard against it.

No Time for Risk Analysis exposes you to reckless risk,
and plants the seeds of mistaking activity for progress.
Be careful what you sow.
What was your answer to question 3 in Chapter 2?

Sources:
1. David P. Snyder, *How to Mind-Read Your Customers*, 2001, 27.

Chapter 9

Mistake 6
Confidence Without Competence

Confidence fuels our drive to take on risks, challenges and to discover. Competence enables us to do so efficiently and effectively. Trouble sets in when there is a mismatch between confidence and competence. Risk Management as a subject is *not a part of the curriculum* in a *majority* of the academic institutions. Neither have *most* business organizations taken the time to formally educate or train their employees in the topic. As a result, competence in Risk Management is sorely lacking, and blissful ignorance prevails. The matrix in Figure 3 Confidence vs Competence illustrates four possible outcomes, and we will study these further in the context of risk management.

	High Confidence	Low Confidence
High Competence	1	2
Low Competence*	3	4

Figure 3. Confidence vs Competence
*Assuming that the person, team, or organization is not aware of this

49

Quadrant 1: Ideal place to be. Confidence will generate action, and competence will ensure risk management gets done right.

Quadrant 2: Difficulty in starting on risk management due to low confidence, however, once started it gets done properly.

Quadrant 3: Dangerous, a propensity for reckless risk taking. Confidence will drive the action, however, lack of competence will result in incomplete or incorrect analysis.

Quadrant 4: Possibly a non-starter due to low confidence, and the lack of competence compounds the situation. Risk management is unlikely to get done at all, and if started will lead to chaos.

Which Quadrant are you in? How do you know?

Only one quadrant provides assurance of success in risk management. This means there is a 75% chance (assuming each Quadrant is equally likely) that risk management will not get done properly. Don't let the simplicity of this matrix belie what actually happens in organizations of just about any size, as the following example illustrates.

Luck runs out In 2003, the space shuttle Columbia disintegrated during re-entry into the earth's atmosphere. Many called it an accident; was it? Investigation pointed to damage on the leading edge of the shuttle's wing, which impaired its ability to withstand high temperatures during re-entry. This damage occurred during take-off when insulating foam hit the wing and damaged heat-shielding tiles on the leading edge, creating a crater. Strangely enough, the phenomenon of insulating foam coming off had happened routinely in the past. That over 100 missions preceding this one did not result in loss of life was sheer luck! One must wonder, despite the repeated incidents of foam coming loose, where did the confidence to launch shuttle missions come from?

Several observations during the investigation pointed to lack of competence in NASA's culture and staff, with regard to overall management of the Shuttle Program and its safety. Here are five observations from the *Columbia Accident Investigation Report.*[1,2,3]

1. Boeing engineers failed in their oversight duties during crater analysis from foam strikes. NASA knew of the phenomenon and had a mitigation plan in place to deal with it; however, it was incomplete, and the training of personnel responsible for such analysis was not uniform.

2. Safety and Mission Assurance organizations supporting the Shuttle Program are largely dependent on the program for funding, which hampers their status as independent observers.

3. Over the last two decades, little or no progress has been made toward attaining integrated, independent, and detailed analysis of risk to the Space Shuttle System.

4. Important system safety engineering and management departments are separated from mainstream engineering. They do not have vigorous impact on system design, and are hidden in the other safety disciplines at NASA headquarters.

5. Managers in the Shuttle Program denied the requests of the Debris Assessment Team investigating the loss of Columbia for access to imagery. They thereby put the team in the untenable position of having to prove that a safety of flight issue existed.

When successes occur despite lackadaisical or improper actions and work habits, a sense of invulnerability, and over confidence takes root. Not only individuals fall victim to this, but also entire organizations and communities do. Many successful companies and their executive teams that I have worked with form such opinions, and once set they are very hard to change. This difficulty comes from two main reasons.

First, people have a hard time accepting that they could be wrong, particularly when historical evidence points the other way. Second, the sense of pride and the ego that comes from previous successes keeps them from seeing reality.

Confidence with competence, Quadrant 1, is hard to beat, however, staying in this quadrant takes effort, awareness, and above all, a willingness and openness to look at things objectively on an ongoing basis. Remember, the transition from High Confidence, High Competence (Quadrant 1) to High Confidence, Low Competence (Quadrant 3) can occur surreptitiously. Additionally, this shift can take place because of someone's willful action, or just because change is built into nature, as the Gita, a Hindu philosophical text tells us, "Change is a rule of nature." The rapid pace of man-made change hastens this transition, and blunts our competence faster than we think. Regardless, there is no excuse for being asleep while awake.

Confidence and competence: While both are needed,
the knowledge of what you have and
what you don't have is even more important.
What was your answer to question 4 in Chapter 2?

Sources:
1.   http://caib.nasa.gov/news/report/pdf/vol1/full/caib_report_volume1.pdf
     page 190
2.   Ibid, page 191
3.   Ibid, page 193

Chapter 10

Mistake 7
Ignoring the Time and Space Dimensions

Edward Lorenz, a pioneer in climate modeling, developed the theory that small changes in initial conditions can cause complex (non-linear dynamic) systems to exhibit large variations over time. This is often referred to as the butterfly effect, which suggests that the flapping of a butterfly's wings in Brazil can cause a tornado in Texas. Could this happen? Can tiny events in one place and time really morph into mega events later at another place? The understanding of how cause and effect are connected in *The Time and Space Dimensions* is not always clear, however, more disturbing is the fact that this connection is often ignored.

Tracing the cause Let's take the following as an example. In 1989, the revenues of a rapidly growing Texas company soared past $35 million mark, but losses due to scrap from furnace operations exceeded a record $1 million. This direct hit of about three percent to the bottom line did not bode well for a company about to go public.

As a result, the company launched frantic efforts to reduce or eliminate scrap. They formed several work teams to attack the problem, looking for causes at their plant. Several tools and techniques were deployed: *Cause and Effect Diagrams* to identify known and potential causes; *Check Sheets* to study the frequency of defect occurrences; *Quantitative Methods* to establish correlations between cause and effect; and *Five Whys* to drill deeper. All of these methods were used in an effort to determine root causes. However, despite their best efforts, they made little progress.

The original cause, lost in memory, had occurred more than five years earlier in a plant in California. The old timers who were familiar with the product knew this, but they were either no longer with the company, or had moved on to other roles. According to them, during the early stages of research and development on furnace operations, defects in materials and process steps had surfaced. However, under pressures to meet deadlines, products were launched, and it was decided to re-visit the troubling issues in the next two quarters, which never happened. (Can you guess which mistake they committed here?) The result was a problem that grew over time, to become a burning issue at a different place, many years later. Such thinking and behavior is all too common throughout many organizations, large and small. Knowledge of true causes is lost because key people move on, or the knowledge gets buried below subsequent layers of events and activities.

Oblivious to what transpired five years ago in California, the company decided on a very expensive option: to change their technology and recover the costs for the same by increasing prices. The market accepted this for a while, however, increased competition resulted in a demise of this product line for the division, and affected the fortunes of the whole corporation.

When analyzing failures or non-conformances, a popular tool called the Cause and Effect Diagram is often used. It is in the form of a fish, the head represents the non-conformance (the What), while the causes (the Whys) are placed on the spine as shown in Figure 4. Convenient for brain storming, and getting teams focused on the problem, this diagram also serves to group causes into a few main categories—typically The Six Ms.

In Figure 4, each of the six main branches represents a

category of causes: Man, Material, Methods, Measurement, Machines, and Mother Nature. Within each category, are listed subsequently deeper causes, as shown. Consider the non-conformance of late deliveries to a customer.

The first Why may yield the answer *"Late to work."* The causative chain takes us to deeper causes such as waking up late, forgetting to set the alarm, etc. In this case, as long as the second level, and deeper causes lie within the same category, (in this case Man) it works fine. When dependence spans categories, the Cause and Effect Diagram has trouble depicting the linkages. For example, suppose being late to work resulted from the car moving slowly, which is related to the route taken, and a heavy downpour. These causes are located under Machines, Methods, and Mother Nature. The Cause and Effect diagram cannot illustrate these cross category dependencies.

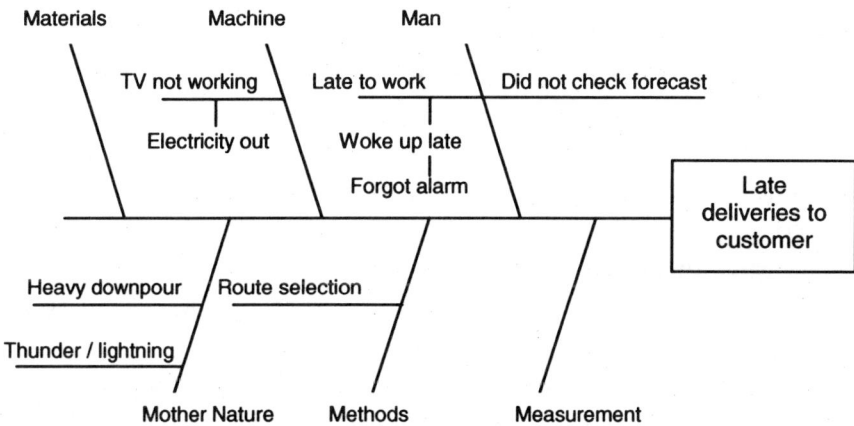

Figure 4. The Cause and Effect Diagram

This inadequacy results in poorly investigated chain of events, causes, and their relationships, especially in complex systems. When left uncorrected, the analysis proceeds down the wrong path, confusing activity with progress, and a false sense of security

55

follows because people think they have found the cause and resolved it. Can you figure out which mistake is a natural outcome of such analysis?

In another case, a team investigated the causes of defects in a medical prosthesis. We ended up looking at the machine shop that manufactured the implant and made changes to their tooling. The problem disappeared for a few weeks, but soon reappeared. In fact, we found the true cause at a much deeper level, at the plant that produced the billets, or raw stock, of titanium metal. The team took nearly seven months to isolate the flawed materials, quarantine them, and locate the true causes which had occurred at a different time in a different place.

Now consider the following as something that could happen to any of us. As the holiday season draws closer, you see an ad on TV with a special offer. You think of the item as an excellent, affordable gift for your brother. You pick up the phone to place the order; the operator very courteously takes your information, and gives you a confirmation number for the credit card transaction.

A few weeks later, your brother calls you, very much pleased with the gift. That same week you get a call from your credit card company. The customer representative says, "Your card has some suspicious activity, and is at its maximum credit limit. You need to send funds."

Bewildered, you ask, "How can this be?"

Could this happen to you? See item 13, in Chapter 17, *What Lies Ahead? 30 Trends or Events to Watch.* When the customer representative recounts the last five charges on your credit card, you realize that they are all false. You are told an investigation will be conducted, and any fraudulent charges may be removed, but it will take time. For now you are stuck with an unusable credit card.

Ignoring the Time and Space Dimension creates alibis that can set you up! Many conventional tools cannot discover the relationship. What did you answer to question 14 in Chapter 2?

Chapter 11

Mistake 8
Tip of the Iceberg – Are You on a Titanic?

Imagine yourself standing at the bow of a ship looking out into the distance. In the faint light of the night sky, you see an object directly in the path of the ship. Is it an iceberg or an island? How long should you wait before you ask the crew to steer away? Should you request them to slow down? Should you ask for another opinion? Will the crew take your alert seriously? Are you crying wolf? Are your eyes playing tricks on you? All sorts of questions race through your mind. Meanwhile, the object draws closer, and there are no clues on what lurks below the surface.

Presented with the evidence of damage to the Columbia during take-off, the shuttle program managers wrestled with similar questions. Should we get detailed images of the shuttle from space satellites? Should we ask the astronauts to conduct a space walk to examine the damage?

In the early 90s I spoke to a group of managers and executives of Sulzermedica, a large international corporation, at the conclusion of a mission and vision building event. Having returned from a recent trip to India, where I had seen the beginnings of a massive change first-hand. I spoke about what the coming two decades would bring. I declared that India will grow into a rising power to reckon with, (see sidebar on Important changes in India) and that the West will feel the pressure from these changes. No one believed me. How could they? The tip of the iceberg was too small, obscure, and in their blind spot.

> **Important changes in India – early 1990s**
> - Relaxation of government controls
> - Opening up of the economy
> - Surprisingly, privatization of state run industries
> - Rising exports
> - A healthy trend in trade balance
> - An ambitious and educated workforce

Back to the ship. Not one to take chances, you signal the captain. He agrees with you, and orders the crew to steer right. As you see the ship turn, you breathe a sigh of relief. The ship will avoid the collision and steer clear of the iceberg. Will it?

Consider these facts:

❖ Ninety percent of an iceberg is typically under water.
❖ You cannot infer the shape of an iceberg below the water from what you see. It can have many other peaks sub-surface.
❖ Icebergs are not static; they can and do move.
❖ Invisible undercurrents can move your ship.

Because of these factors, seeing the tip of the iceberg and taking evasive action may not be enough to mitigate risk, or steer clear of danger.

A multi-billion dollar, world-leading manufacturer of computing equipment had a sterling reputation among consumers and corporate customers. The company produced high quality PCs, but they were priced out of the range of many individual users. Over time, cheaper copycat models flooded the market, and margins in the PC business dropped significantly. Seeing the problem with an iceberg perspective, the company decided to change course. They sold the PC division, and focused on high-end workstations, and servers.

However, they failed to recognize under currents in those markets. Neither did they pay attention to the ease with which a competitor could leap from making PCs to making servers and high-end workstations. This was common knowledge to the engineers, however it lay in the blind spot for key decision makers in the organization. Even larger problems were present sub-surface. They recognized (too late) that the major issues were related to operational inefficiencies within the whole company, rather than just the PC division (*The Tip of the Iceberg*).

The world stood ready to buy more computers, but not at the prices they offered. Their competitors, on the other hand, negotiated with suppliers and built in price cuts for components at the rate of 5 to 15 percent per year, keeping pace with erosion of selling prices. The competition took into account not only the iceberg, but its shifting position as well, and responded with automatic shifts to their course.

The Tip Of The Iceberg – The true magnitude of the problem is often ten times worse than what is visible on the surface. Further, problems may not remain static. What was your answer to question 7 in Chapter 2?

Chapter 12

Mistake 9
Mixing up Signal and Noise

Signal is defined as anything that serves to indicate, warn, direct, or command. Noise, on the other hand, is irrelevant, meaningless information. While noise is omnipresent, signals are often fleeting; they come and go. Both exist. In most cases, it is possible to identify the unique cause or causes for signals. Weak signals may need amplification so they can be detected. Noise defies easy analysis. More importantly, too many signals present at the same time can *appear* as noise.

Our responses   We as individuals and organizations are conditioned to respond to signals, and have learned to ignore noise for the most part. Furthermore, when signals persist for a long time, they can give the impression of being noise. Some of the factors that affect signal detection are:

- ❖ The level of noise.
- ❖ The periodicity of the signal, noise, and detector operation.
- ❖ Effectiveness of the detection system.

Trouble starts when we mistake signal for noise or vice versa. Figure 5 shows four outcomes associated with Perceptions and the Truth about Signals vs. Noise.

	Perception	
	Signal	Noise
Truth		
Signal	1	2
Noise	3	4

Figure 5. Outcomes of Perception vs. Truth

Each outcome bears further examination.

Outcome 1:

Signal is interpreted correctly, and this is the ideal state. Appropriate risk management and corrective actions can be implemented based on this outcome. However, an understanding of how quickly signals get detected after the occurrence of the cause, and how long before corrective action can address the cause is critical.

Outcome 2:

We interpret Signal as Noise, and therefore ignore it. This results in failure to act when we should, and causes high risk.

Examples:
- Intelligence organizations perceive events preceding 9/11 as noise and take no specific action.
- Stock price changes are attributed to random fluctuations in the market. No action is taken.
- Global warming is looked upon as the usual variation in temperature over centuries, and therefore ignored.

Outcome 3:

We see a Signal, while in fact it is Noise. In this case, we take action when we shouldn't.

Examples:

- People of a certain race are singled out for extra scrutiny even though they have a clean record.
- Stock price changes are mistaken as being caused by actions, such as advertising of a product, rather than routine market fluctuations. (This actually led a company to double its advertising budget.)
- Global warming is attributed to special causes such as methane from certain farm animals, and the government orders their extermination.

Outcome 4:

We see Noise for what it really is. There is nothing wrong with this. The choice to do risk management or not depends on the situation, and whether we can reliably detect and act upon the causes for this noise. Improvement in the Signal to Noise Ratio is desirable; this requires reduction in noise levels.

Misunderstandings between signal and noise can result from several reasons. Some of them are as follows:

- Not knowing enough about the system, process or product.
- Lack of training or awareness of what to look for.
- Deliberate attempt at increasing noise level to obscure the signals.
- Use of inadequate or incorrect measurement systems.
- Relying on human memory.

Convenient recall Human memory deserves some elaboration; it is not as reliable as we think, even when data is available. What we remember, or choose to remember, depends on several factors such as relevance, immediacy (how quickly events will likely impact us), the gravity of the experience with the event, and frequency of occurrence. This list, though not exhaustive, assumes there are no pathological or other neurological conditions creating impairment in brain function and memory.

For analyzing hard to detect signals mixed with noise, you may have to rely on the use of sophisticated technology to separate out traceable causes. For instance, use of statistical analysis software and filters can enable data mining to ferret out the signals and their causes.

Measurement systems also play an important role; inadequacy in these can add to the confusion. Therefore, it is important to know how a measurement system can derail you, especially in this information-intense, data-driven society.   It will serve you well to understand what characteristics are important when it comes to measurement systems. They are as follows:

1. Accuracy

How closely does the measured value, indication, or observation compare to the true value? Inaccuracies create misleading signals and result in wrong decisions, which become difficult or impossible to correct in some cases.

Examples:
- Faulty market intelligence is reported to have led to the launch of products that did not fit well within a particular culture or country. This occurred with a Korean company that launched consumer products in the U.S.
- Friendly fire kills scores of soldiers because of inaccuracy in positional information.
- Inaccurate financial statements lead to erroneous business decisions. Imagine acquiring a company and not knowing about the true financial condition of that company. This occurred with a leading flower distributor in the U.S.

2. Repeatability and Reproducibility

How consistent is the measurement system between people, locations, measuring methods, and instruments, and what happens if the same person uses it repeatedly? Inconsistencies from such factors can lead to varying measurements or observations, when in fact nothing may have changed, creating confusion between signal and noise.

Examples:

- During the 1970s, we made oil seals in our company in Bombay. One of our customers happened to reject a batch, even though these had passed inspection at our end. When we inspected the returned seals again, we found nothing wrong. Therefore, we shipped them back to the customer who accepted them the second time around.

- In numerous blind studies that I have conducted as part of Lean and Six Sigma workshops, over 35 percent of the participants misjudge the brand of the soft drink they are given to taste. This occurred even though the same soft drink was served as the baseline and test specimen during the study.

3. Stability

How stable is the system over time? What if the measurement system drifts? While this may cause problems with both accuracy and consistency, you may not be able to detect it easily in the absence of frequent checks.

Examples:

- For high performance permanent magnet motors, characterizing the magnetic fields is critical. The gauss meter used for this purpose was accurate when calibrated, however it was not known to the magnet manufacturers that the instrument drifted over time. This resulted in wrongly rejecting good magnets over several production lots, impacting profitability for the company.

- In the case of a high tech manufacturing firm, the definition of acceptable product would drift over the course of the quarter. Towards the end of the quarter, borderline performing products and those with certain types of defects would be deemed acceptable. This was done to ensure the firm could meet the shipment deadlines and quarterly quotas. Such behavior in the face of bold statements like "Quality first" sows the seeds of distrust between management and staff. Over time staff learns to ignore the need for making improvements, customers experience the poor quality, and eventually find better alternatives.

Signal and Noise: Both are usually present. The latter obfuscates. What were your answers to questions 4 and 15 in Chapter 2?

Chapter 13

Mistake 10
Rationalization – A Double-Edged Sword

Rationalizing our decisions and actions is natural for us. This follows from our innate desire to understand cause and effect, and distaste for being wrong. Rationalization, has enabled mankind to discover some of the most useful principles of the universe, among them the Theory of Gravity, the Laws of Thermodynamics, Photosynthesis, and several others. However, misguided actions and decisions result when we rationalize habits such as smoking. Arguments that distort risks and benefits get presented; here are some that were used in favor of smoking when I interviewed a random sample of 18 people during an overseas business trip:

> "It helps me to relax and so indirectly, I reap some health benefit."
> "It repels insects."
> "It helps me lose weight."

Finding pros and cons to anything is easy, and therein lays the reason to be careful with rationalization. Speeding, for example, is rationalized by statements such as, "I drive fast, but I am safe," "There are no cops around," and "I am running late." Rationalization for legitimate reasons is understandable, however, malleable thinking and memory make the illegitimate acceptable.

Consider the matrix in Figure 6 that details Events and Preparedness. Four combinations are possible, and we will discuss each briefly.

	Known Event	Unknown Event
Prepared	Minimal risk	Very good
Unprepared	In-excusable	Depend on luck!

Figure 6. Events vs Preparedness

Prepared for the Known

Being prepared for the known is a good situation to be in. It is usually the outcome of due diligence, however, it is no reason to celebrate.

Example:

A computer manufacturer decides to sell products in Southeast Asia and preliminary research on consumer behavior indicates they will continue to use their machines under brownout conditions. The manufacturer decides to use power supplies that can withstand large variations in supply voltage.

Prepared for the Unknown

Being prepared for the unknown is very good. So good it leads us to ask if this was a fluke, or the result of extra diligence. Either way, you are prepared for surprises.

Example:

The same computer manufacturer happens to have a dust and moisture resistant keyboard on their machines. They *did not know* that in many parts of Southeast Asia, highly dusty conditions are normal, and during monsoons, considerable amounts of condensation can take place as well.

Unprepared for the Known

Of the four conditions, being unprepared for the known is the hardest to justify, yet in reality it is the most frequently rationalized using arguments such as, "We couldn't have seen it coming."

Example:

A cell phone manufacturer tries to sell their products in third world countries at U.S. prices. The market simply cannot bear this, and sales do not take off. The marketing group concludes the countries in the region are not ready for cell phones, and therefore no other manufacturer would care to enter the market. This despite the fact that public phone call boxes were common place, and very profitable, and satellite TVs were common place in the poorest neighborhoods in the country. Out of the box thinkers saw the opportunity and stepped in to grab the market. One of the world's fastest growing cell phone markets went to competitors!

Unprepared for the Unknown

Being unprepared for the unknown is easy to explain using arguments similar to those presented in the previous case, "We couldn't see it coming." However, many things are "knowable." The real question is why was it unknown? Because of inadequate investigation, diligence, and probing? Or, because some things are truly unknowable? The latter fall under the category *"only God knows"* and can possibly be excused. Advancements in science and technology keep shifting the boundary between knowable and truly unknowable.

Example:

Heavy rains lashed Mumbai, on the western coast of India on July 26, 2005. The city received about 25 inches of rain in 12 hours, and a record 37 inches in a 24 hour period. The previous record was about 23 inches in 24 hours. It is estimated that 1000 people lost their lives.[3] Flooding in the city is common during the monsoon season, and a high tide makes matters worse. When this occurs, the city gets paralyzed, all traffic comes to a standstill, and the airport also shuts down. Just how much rain will pour, and when? What will be the extent of the damage? *Only God knows.*

Does this mean we should not do anything, and rationalize the status quo, or inaction? If that were done, what would that lead to?

Rationalization: Can lead to irrational thinking, decisions, and behaviors. Be careful, it cuts both ways! What did you answer to question 7 in Chapter 2?

Sources:
1. http://www.usfa.dhs.gov/downloads/pdf/tfrs/v4i4.pdf
2. http://eweek.com/article2/0,1895,1628348,00.asp
3. http://en.wikipedia.org/wiki/2005_Maharashtra_floods

Summary of the Ten Mistakes

Let us take a few minutes to revisit the ten mistakes with the understanding that these are not the only ones. Here they are.

Mistake 1, The Terribility Factor
High severity events or situations cause emotions to reach an extreme point where rational thinking ceases. As we over react, or over compensate, we ignore existing risks and create new ones in the process.

Mistake 2, Recency and Frequency
The influence of recent or frequently occurring events builds cumulative psychological trauma, bringing us to a snapping point. The result again, is loss of rational thinking, followed by overreaction or overcompensation.

Mistake 3, The Illusion of Control
The mistaken belief that things are under control or that we can control them, when in reality, it is not so. This leads to erroneous decisions and actions, increasing risk.

Mistake 4, The Trap of Comfort Zones
Trapper habits and behaviors both make us comfortable, and complacent. The result is ignored signals, slow responses, and increased risk.

Mistake 5, No Time for Risk Analysis
A constant feeling of being rushed causes us to focus more on activity rather than doing meaningful risk analysis.

Mistake 6, Confidence without Competence

The erroneous belief, and over confidence, that things will workout in our favor. It pre-disposes us to take reckless risks rather than being prudent.

Mistake 7, Ignoring the Time and Space Dimension

Studying cause and effect without consideration of time and space. This leads to faulty analysis and focus on the wrong risk factors.

Mistake 8, Tip of the Iceberg

Seeing the tip of the iceberg, we think we know what the risks are, however, majority of the risks lie under the surface. This mistake leads us astray like no other.

Mistake 9, Mixing up Signal and Noise

Mistaking one for the other, we either take faulty action or no action at all. As a result, real risks go undetected and may even magnify.

Mistake 10, Rationalization – A Double-Edged Sword

Rationalizing leads us to justify everything, including wrong actions, and behaviors. The resulting paradigms can leave us ill prepared to deal with known risks.

Now it is your turn to sharpen your skills in detecting these mistakes using the exercises provided in the next chapter.

Exercises for Part II

These exercises are meant to build your skill at spotting which mistake is occurring or is about to occur. Building this skill helps prevent the mistakes from happening. Keeping the *Ten Mistakes* in perspective, carefully study each situation or scenario. All exercises are based on or adapted from real life situations.

Exercise 1: (Personal)
For the past three months, your daughter has been applying to colleges for admission. She has filled out all the forms and written essays to accompany each application. Critical submission dates are coming closer, yet in the middle of all of this, she maintains her part time job, a regular class schedule including routine homework and tests, and she participates in three extracurricular activities. Her day begins at 6:30 a.m. and ends around 1 a.m.

Because of this hectic schedule, she has little time for socializing. Her friends have withdrawn from her lately, and she finds herself somewhat isolated. However, she has kept up with the workload and boasts that few others could handle so much. You as the parent know of at least two previous incidents when she has undertaken challenges without adequate preparation: competing in the spelling bee, and running in a 10K race without adequate physical conditioning.

Exercise 2: (Manufacturer)
A large manufacturer of tires as original equipment has been in business for over fifty years. There has never been a recall of

any product in the company's history, and they have a very close relationship with two leading car manufacturers. Design engineers of these companies and the tire manufacturer work closely as new models are conceptualized and advance through the phases to launch.

Consumers have reported isolated cases of a recent SUV model (less than two years old) overturning on the highways. Collision was not identified as the cause in any of the incidents. This has never happened to any of the models before. In every case of overturned SUVs, they found damage to one or more tires. The drivers who survived these incidents report that the vehicle just started swaying, and they lost control of it.

Warranty claims at the car dealerships or the tire manufacturer's chain of stores have not shown any change from norms. Both the tire and car manufacturer speculated on possible causes and conclude that the cause must have been a wind gust, some other weather related phenomena, or the drivers were speeding. Engineers at the car company knew that the center of gravity of this SUV was higher than all previous models. In light of that, the car company issued a bulletin to all its dealerships to reduce the tire pressure to lower the center of gravity. This was added to the procedure for preparing cars for Pre-Delivery Inspection. The procedures and the user manual were updated before the SUV was launched in the market, and customers were instructed to keep the pressures lower.

Exercise 3: (Business Service Provider)

A2Z Inc. is an international business process outsourcing company based in Europe and wants to offer its services to a client in Germany. Its client has operations all over Europe and provides insurance for homes and automobiles to consumers. Competitive pressures are mounting for the client and they have decided to outsource some of their work to low-cost regions through A2Z. The type of work that is being considered for outsourcing has to do with fielding calls related to the customer's property and automobiles. This will include collecting personal information from clients.

A2Z will subcontract most of its work to a company in India or China. In both countries, its contacts have assured that they can meet its requirements. A2Z has not met with the actual service providers; nor has it spoken with any of the customer service representatives. The date for signing the contract with its client is only four days away, and its client is pressing A2Z to signup or the opportunity will be lost. The next one may be more than a year out. A2Z's client will be shutting down in-house call centers in less than a month from now.

Exercise 4: (Government)

One of the cities (RK) in a southwestern state of a G8 nation has a spectacular record of maintaining safety levels for its citizens. The city has been recognized for this, and other cities have emulated RK's performance.

As word of the bird flu spreads, many coastal cities began preparations thinking that the migrating birds would bring it to their shores. So far, no incident of bird flu had occurred, but the migratory patterns of the birds have been known for several decades, and these birds have been sighted in RK occasionally in the past.

During several staff meetings, the topic of preparing the city for bird flu had come up. However, preoccupation with routine matters and the preparations for upcoming baseball games always pushed the discussion aside.

The city's chief engineer responsible for risk analysis claimed that because their city lies more than 150 miles from the coast, they should not face the problem. Even if one or two birds stray that far, he reasoned, it shouldn't concern them. They would quarantine any such bird.

Some argued that this did not amount to adequate precaution

and that the city needed to be pro-active in managing this risk. To this, the chief engineer replied, "We can't chase everything that has a remote possibility of doing us harm. If we try, our regular jobs will never get done."

This remark coming from an authority with an impeccable safety record was enough assurance for the rest of the staff, and they considered the matter resolved.

Exercise 5: (U.S. Corporation–NASDAQ Listed)

AM, Corp. is about to acquire a smaller competitor TM to get market share in an area where AM has no presence. The primary driving factors include the high level of respect TM enjoys with its customers, and the fact that it has an established history in the market. TM also has a 3 percent market share in a $700 million market. AM views the acquisition of TM as an important step because it would acquire all the product designs and know-how at a reasonable price. Although TM has not shown a profit, AM's management thinks the acquisition can help through economies of scale and streamlining of processes. This in turn can yield as much as 6 percent to the bottom line over the years.

TM has capitalized on six products and AM has the wherewithal to study them in detail. Both companies have similar skill sets, except that AM is four times the size of TM. When AM engineers studied TM's products, they found them complicated and cumbersome for production. Moreover, two of the six have had some field incidents that the company has not acted on so far.

The news of this acquisition of TM and AM has generated considerable euphoria among shareholders and employees of both companies. They all agree that the acquisition should move forward. The board of directors has recommended a speedy closing as well. Since AM's stock has significantly appreciated in the recent past, it can easily afford this acquisition. Executives and the board make the final decision to close the deal in about two months.

Exercise 6: (Human Capacity for Estimating)

You may want to take this test with your co-workers. Draw three lines of different lengths, each between 4" and 9" long. Label them as Line 1, Line 2, and Line 3. Then follow instructions exactly as shown, recording values to the nearest 0.5mm (or 1/32" if using inches). Do not share results until instructed.

1. Measure lines 1, 2, and 3 yourself. Write down the answer, do not disclose.
2. Have two (or more) people do step 1 – without disclosing the measurements to each other.
3. Have two groups of people *estimate* the length of the lines without disclosing the answer to each other. It is a good idea to have one group start with the longer line and proceed to the shorter one, and others do the reverse.
4. After everyone completes their measurements, compare notes.

NOTE: Do not have the participants announce the answers at any time. Collect their notes and study their answers.

What are the differences among the participants' measurements of the lines? For step 3 above, how did the measurements differ between the groups?

Common to all the exercises is the human element. In its absence, the question of mistakes does not arise, so let's take some time to understand more about the human element. A study of Risk Management without such an understanding would be incomplete. After all, the key to success in any endeavor is understanding how to prevent failures.

Part III

What You Can Do

Chapter 14

How Capable are We?
Understanding the Human Dimension

We commonly describe risk as the exposure to injury or loss. Because many think of it in abstract terms, risk is often misunderstood. Furthermore, tolerance for risk varies significantly. As a result, we exacerbate mistakes in decisions and actions. This indicates a significant inconsistency in how we comprehend risk. Therefore, it behooves us to study the human dimension at length.

Understanding what makes us who we are, and the influence of the environment we live in are vital in this effort. We will begin by looking at what happened in several cases where individuals and groups encountered and responded to risk. This will shed more light on why people and organizations behave the way they do.

Return on Ignorance, Intelligence, or Intuition?

In the moments before the tsunami hit (on the morning of December 26, 2004) the coastal areas of Indonesia, some people noticed that the sea had receded too far from the beach. Curiosity drove them to explore this unusual phenomenon. On the other hand, when the village's tribal elders saw the sea recede, they moved their folks to safer havens. A little later, as huge waves approached, curiosity drove tourists closer to the beach to see the awesome waves coming ashore. They moved closer to the water to get a better view and capture the event on video. In one case, curiosity-driven actions saved lives; in the other, it jeopardized lives. The difference between the two situations was Risk Management.

Since organizations are comprised of people, anomalous behavior is to be expected from the organization. Take the case of NASA; the sense of tolerable risk (from the foam debris that came off during every launch) increased because no safety of flight issues occurred in over 100 missions. When luck ran out with the Columbia tragedy in 2003, the paradigm of acceptable risk changed drastically. We can trace similar thinking back to the 1986 Challenger incident[2] and to the 1967 Apollo launch pad fire.[3] That happened in an organization made of smart professionals with strong credentials.

Here is an example with people from the general populace. Table saw mishaps cause about 60,000 people to lose fingers every year in the U.S. These injuries change people's lives and society incurs costs such as medical expenses, lost wages, worker's compensation, increased insurance rates, lost productivity, etc. to the tune of $2 billion! Yet, when Dr. Stephen Gass introduced fail-safe technology to prevent these injuries, not a single saw manufacturer was willing to incorporate it into their designs. The reason the saw manufacturers declined to use this technology was they couldn't figure out how to make money from it. Eventually, Dr. Gass[4] ended up starting his own company manufacturing safe table saws under the name of "Saw Stop."

In the case of the tsunami, we must ask if the tourists were being brave, stupid, or ignorant. We wonder if tribal elders acted out of deliberation, or instinct. Did fate play a role in all of this? Did the concept of acceptable risk lull managers at NASA into ignoring the danger signs? Did no one sound the alarm? No! Of course alarms were sounded and concerns were raised, but either no one heard it, or no one chose to act despite the alarms. Recall from the Introduction that only 8% of those who hear fire alarms go off take them seriously.

Whether we call it return on ignorance, intelligence, or intuition, everyone involved had different perceptions of the risk they faced. In the case of the tsunami incident, the tourists didn't know of the risk lurking behind the receding waters and the huge waves that followed. Forget about analysis. Once the waves closed in, there was no time for analysis anyway. The tourists had no experience or knowledge of such phenomena, therefore, matters were left purely to chance. In the case of NASA, investigation showed that analysis was conducted, but other factors overrode any concern of risk and they were at the mercy of luck again. The choice to do nothing in the face of risk prevailed, but it was the wrong choice.

Cost of irrationality If you still think people behave rationally in large business deals, think again. From new ventures to business acquisitions and expansions, the process of risk analysis is primitive, if done at all. Because of this, many new businesses fail in the first year of operation, and less than half make it past five years (see Case Study 4). In addition, a vast majority of mergers and acquisitions fail to deliver the promised efficiencies.

Governments and corporations all over the world spend hundreds of billions every year, launching initiatives with great fanfare. The initiatives deliver spectacular results in very few instances, however, most produce mediocre outcomes, and this is nothing new. Yet, in how many of these organizations is "any" risk analysis conducted before the initiative? The answer may surprise you. If you haven't noticed it, maybe the next time you hear of an initiative being launched at your place of work, quietly observe if they do risk analysis. You will see why a potential sizzle ends up as a fizzle.

The Human Species

As a species, our DNA is over 98 percent similar to the genetic material of apes and chimpanzees. We may feel that humans have roamed the planet for a long time, approximately two million years, however, we are still the "new kids on the block."

No other species can match our accomplishments. We went from homes of caves and huts of straw to living in well-built high-rise buildings of steel and glass. Our locomotion went from walking and running to jet-setting across continents. Long distance communication went from pounding on drums and sending smoke signals to instant digital communication over phones and the Internet with anyone, anytime, and anywhere on the planet.

On the negative side, the way we fight went from close quarters combat to remotely launched weapons of mass destruction using consoles reminiscent of video games.

The way we take in information, interpret concepts, and make decisions, all influence how we deal with risk. Several factors come into play, of which we will explore the following five:

1. Nature and the role of evolution
2. Nurture and human conditioning
3. Complexity in products and services
4. The business world today
5. Fear and emotion

1. Nature and the Role of Evolution

For the most part, nature gave us instinct programmed behaviors such as the fight or flight response, the tendency to seek equilibrium, the curiosity to explore, and motivation. Let us probe each of these.

Fight or flight response When faced with imminent danger, the fight or flight response works as a lifesaver by enabling us to act without thinking. However, the sudden rise in adrenaline levels leads to "knee-jerk" reactionary moves that are harmful under certain conditions. For example: trying to steer a skidding car. Most people end up steering harder in the direction they want to turn, or they panic and hit the brakes making the situation worse. Actually, the only way to regain control of the car is to steer into the skid, and *not* slam the brakes. Both are totally counterintuitive moves. Technology has come to the rescue, and provided us the anti-lock brake system, therefore in this case the damage from slamming the brakes is reduced.

Compare this with what happens when you touch a hot iron by mistake. To prevent burns, your hand jerks away without thinking. Similarly, the rapid response works for a person losing their balance. Instinctively, the arms stretch out, adjusting posture to regain balance and control.

The same fight or flight response results in two very different outcomes. In one case, it increases risk; in the other, it mitigates risk.

Tendency to Seek Equilibrium Nature has a built-in *tendency* to attain equilibrium both in our physical and mental states. This applies to just about every aspect of personal and business life. It operates at all levels and functions including physiological and psychological, and spans from cellular to overall body function. Earlier we discussed the water drop, however, it was inanimate.

For any system to operate in equilibrium (or steady state), it needs sensors, set points, feedback loops, and corrective action when necessary. Sensors detect the imbalance and when it exceeds a certain threshold, the system initiates corrective action to restore equilibrium. The above examples amply illustrate this point. The tendency to seek equilibrium applies equally well to decision making.

We find dealing with the unpleasant, such as potential failures, painful and difficult. However, despite our best efforts, certain situations carry a degree of risk in which the threat does not go away. When risk continues for some time without an incident, we tend to rationalize and live with the threat. Doing so increases our sense of comfort and equilibrium in the face of threats or risks that persist. This begins to build the confidence that nothing will go wrong, and we end up being unprepared for the expected.

Such thinking also puts us in the situation of Confidence without Competence—Quadrant 3, Figure 3. We break through that false sense of security only when the possibility of failure turns into reality, such as in the loss of the space shuttle, or having field failures in a product that had minimal to no risk evaluation early in the life cycle. Only then do we justify corrective and preventive measures, putting them into place and regaining our sense of equilibrium. Strangely, these same preventive measures may have been previously dismissed as being impractical or too expensive. What was once irrational now appears rational.

On the one hand, this tendency to seek a state of equilibrium helps us reduce stress. On the other, it can make us complacent through the creation of a comfort zone. The latter eventually leads us astray as we begin overlooking risks; this afflicts individuals regardless of education or experience.

Curiosity to explore, and motivation Nearly every species seeks stimulation, and this is why we explore. How far we venture in exploration is most often determined by the reward, the

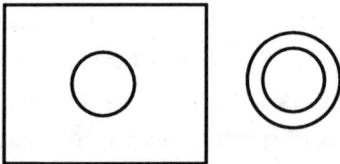

Which inner circle is bigger?

Figure 7. Checking Sensory Ability

uncertainty, and the threat to self-preservation associated with it. While our senses provide the input for such decisions, we cannot always depend on the reliability of our senses. For example, look at the circles in Figure 7. Each inner circle is the same size, however, one seems larger than the other. Consider also, how a mirage can easily trick us into believing there is water out there on the ground, where none exists.

Sensory overload reduces our ability to comprehend and make sound decisions. For example, when you first begin to ride a bicycle (explore), enjoying a song simultaneously is impossible (sensory overload). Your only focus is on maintaining balance to prevent a fall. As your comfort level in balancing the bike increases (steady state), you are able to enjoy music as well.

The motivation for exploration can be intrinsic or extrinsic. Intrinsic motivation drives us to explore with the reward being the exploration itself. Extrinsic motivation drives exploration based on an external reward. This has important consequences, since changes and actions driven primarily on extrinsic motivation will likely be short-lived once the reward is removed or attained, unless the behavior has become habit. Therefore, the type of motivation and the habits that have formed will dictate how much risk analysis gets done.

2. Nurture and Human Conditioning

Our conditioning strongly influences our habits, behaviors, and ability to comprehend risk. Of the several factors that play an important role in behaviors influenced by Nurture, we will focus on the following four:

> Information that comes to us passes through different filters, whether we are aware of it or not. These filters form due to several factors including upbringing, culture, education, training, and so forth. Hence, the knowledge we carry has some bias to begin with.

❖ Paradigms
❖ Perceptions
❖ Use of rules
❖ Understanding cause and effect

Although in the early formative years we have little control over what we experience, this situation changes significantly as we grow up. Therefore, we cannot totally lay blame on, or give credit to our parents or guardians for what we become. Let us take a deeper look into the four factors now.

Paradigms If you needed a pacemaker, and the state's health care system offered an unknown, cheaper brand, one made in a non-descript country vs. one made in Japan, would you accept the cheaper one? Why or why not?

During my pre-teen years in the late 1950s, my father bought me a very nice bicycle. It came with a battery operated horn and several other accessories. Unfortunately, within a month many of the accessories broke down. Dismayed, I told him about the horn, and the lights not working.

He looked over the bike, and said, "Son, these are cheap Japanese products, what can we expect? Look, the bicycle itself is made in England. See how robust it is? Let's get some accessories made in England, Germany, or USA."

His comments created an impression in my mind that lasted well into the mid 1970s. Every time I bought something, I checked the label for country of origin. Some time during the 1970s, I saw many of my friends opting for Japanese products. The earliest one that comes to mind is a Hitachi transistor radio, a sleek little piece of technology that worked very well.

I saw better quality in Japanese products repeatedly. One day, I found my Enfield Bullet 350cc motorcycle, an Indian version of the British design, no match for a 250cc Japanese bike. Moreover, the frequency of repairs on my bike was two to three times higher. Since behaviors and opinions die hard, I stuck with my paradigms regarding Japanese products all the way into the 1980s.

We all carry internal frameworks that we use as reference points. When we receive information of any type, we react by comparing it with our internal references. If there is none, the decision to accept, reject, or modify the information may be influenced by the urgency of our needs. With an available internal reference (familiarity), we find it easier to make an accept/reject decision. Marketing experts often rely on the *familiar* to induce you to buy something that is *unfamiliar*. According to Jean Piaget[5], a Swiss psychologist, we react to input by "accommodating," and/or "assimilating."

Accommodating involves *adjusting our (internal) understanding,* assimilating involves *modifying the (external) new information* and breaking it down to fit our (internal) understanding. In my view, before this occurs, we make a decision that has even bigger consequences. That has to do with acceptance rejection, or modification of the information based on *automatic processing of the input without pausing to think.*

With rejection, we simply refuse to accept the information as even remotely true and dismiss it outright. When we decide to accept the information, it passes through unique filters and gets colored to varying degrees. Then, the next steps of accommodating or assimilating spring into action. One can lead to the other. Let me give you some examples.

Consider a person whose predictions have often proven false. He now warns you that one of your key customers is about to jump ship. Lack of credibility leads you to discount such statements, and you reject the information outright.

On the other hand, if you received the same information from a trusted friend, you would accept it and react by accommodating or assimilating it. If you chose to accommodate, you would think about how the loss of that client will affect your business and what adjustments you will need to make. If assimilating, you reason that the customer always argued about prices and was overly demanding (internal understanding of what you know). Therefore, their loss may not be a bad thing after all. You may do one, the other, or do both to varying extents.

How we respond—accept, reject, modify—then accommodate, or assimilate—directly affects our approach to risk management.

In the absence of experience, we tend to *accommodate* most of the information we receive. This happens more so when the source is authentic, we are open-minded enough, and conditioned to accept the information as is. Our tendency to *assimilate* new information increases with experience; however, this can become misdirected and harmful if *inappropriate* rationalization sets in.

In any case, after the information is processed through these stages, it goes into building and shaping our paradigms. They create new or adjusted filters, which color our perception of risk. Accommodation or assimilation can also operate complementarily rather than on a mutually exclusive basis. However, one often dominates.

Perceptions Consider these two situations. First, you are meeting with a sales person, and the two of you exchange business cards. While holding your card in his hands, he begins to levitate it in the air. Awestruck, you watch in disbelief as he makes the card gyrate in the air, and brings it to rest gently on his palm. Could this really be happening?

Second, you immerse your hand in freezing water for some time, and then put it in room temperature water. It feels hot, even though the water isn't even warm. Why?

In the first case, the perception is the card levitates, however, this conflicts with your prior knowledge that heavier-than-air objects cannot float in air without external means. In the second case, the perception of the water's hot temperature is relatively true. The hand conditioned itself to a certain environment, and now it has changed significantly. Thus, in the absence of truth (the actual temperature of the water), perception can be, and is, accepted as reality. This happens routinely; for instance, what we *accept as* white light is actually the spectrum of seven colors.

The five senses, together with our paradigms, create perception, which we treat as reality. However, the senses are not always reliable, and it follows that perceptions are likewise.

Flawed perceptions sow the seeds for errors and serious failures. *(What did you answer to question 11 in Chapter 2?)*

A classic example in the business world is the perception that outsourcing is the right thing to do, and so it happens across the board. A Purchasing Manager was overheard saying, "After all, how can you turn down the offer to hire three well-qualified engineers for the price of one?"

However, some companies have reversed their decisions because the total cost of handholding and supporting the new suppliers to get them up to speed far exceeded the real savings. They came to realize that the true costs outweighed the benefits, especially in the cases of immature technologies or industries, and for which the resources in those countries are not yet up to the mark. Meanwhile, thousands of employees in the home country offices were let go, and with them went much of the knowledge that made the company's products work.

The same applies to risk. Consider the following facts and answer the questions posed.

- For the past ten years, Situation A has resulted in 30,000 to 40,000 fatalities per year, and there is nothing in the works to change the situation.

- Situation B has the *potential* of tens of thousands of fatalities, however, only 2,000 are known to have occurred ever. There are strong measures and safety systems in place to prevent loss of life.

Which situation poses a bigger risk, A or B?

Because we will always be influenced and limited by what our senses tell us, we must ensure that we evaluate stimuli accurately, that we consider the context, and remove as much subjectivity as possible. This will improve the Signal to Noise ratio and enhance our ability to detect signals before it is too late.

The sense of being in control and the decay of memories also affects our perceptions of risk. Consider the previous example of riding in a car as a passenger vs. driving it yourself. Most people get anxious while riding in the passenger's seat; however, they feel safer when they are driving. The sense of control when you occupy the driver's seat somehow diminishes the perceived risk, perhaps because you think you can control the outcome. We also perceive the amount of risk in terms of whether we willingly take it on or if it is thrust upon us.

Further, perception is influenced by recency and frequency. The decay of memories erodes the level of awareness that stems from an event as shown in Figure 8, thereby reducing our sensitivity over time, and pre-disposing us to repeating mistakes.

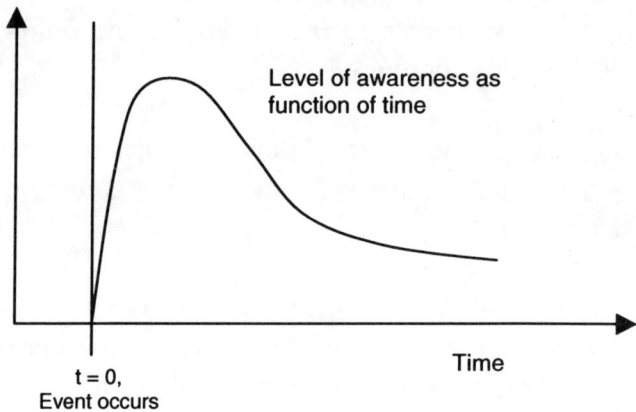

Figure 8. Level of Awareness after an Event.

History cites the troubles Napoleon experienced because of the harsh weather when he invaded Russia during the early 1800s. Hitler underwent a similar fate during 1940s. What occurred during the hurricane of 1900 that hit the city of Galveston, on the Texas coast had been completely lost until Katrina lashed at

92

Louisiana coast during 2005. The memory of Katrina will be forgotten as well since the information explosion continues to pile new experiences and data into human memory. Mankind, therefore, tends to repeat the same mistakes periodically. This results in a loss of the ability to contain risk, unless society or institutions put controls in place. A good example of this is the use of Ground Fault Circuit Interrupters in homes to mitigate the risk of an electrical shock.

Use of rules As we go through life, society programs us to use and obey a variety of rules, both written and unwritten. We quickly learn that following these rules often makes life less complicated. Rules cover a broad spectrum and include everything from the simple need to say, "Please" when asking for something, to complex things such as competing in chess and building airplanes.

	When followed	If not followed
Written Rules	Transparency, and making exceptions is easy to do	Non Conformance
Unwritten Rules	Opacity/Confusion	Unpredictability

Figure 9. Rules and Responses

Organizations too need rules in the forms of policies, procedures, and standards to function effectively, and efficiently. Rules may be written and followed; however, unwritten rules exist, and can be just as powerful. At times, we must make exceptions to the rules. When guided properly (Nurture), we learn how and when to make these exceptions. In other cases, following rules may very well lead us into trouble.

The following is an interesting case of what happens when strictly following rules. It is from a counting class in a remote Asian village. During the class on numbers, the teacher said, "20—twenty, 21— twenty-one, 22—twenty-two," and so on, until he reached "29—twenty-nine." Excited, and in anticipation, a student interrupted, "I know the next number—twenty-ten!"

Although this mistake is benign in nature, such errors in life and in business can have disastrous consequences. What happens, for example, when a person used to driving in the U.S., all of a sudden has to drive in the U.K., or some commonwealth country? Or, while driving your wife's car one day, you turn on the left signal, only to find that the wipers turned on? Could this result in a collision? Would it qualify as an accident?

Examples from business abound. While trying to strike a deal with our company for the sale of a Learning Management System (Database), the sales representative repeatedly pronounced the author's last name as "Kowdhary." Apparently, the first two letters—Ch—followed by the vowel 'o' threw him a curve. Suspecting their ability to provide good customer service, we placed our order with another company.

This representative didn't understand the significance of pronouncing someone's name properly, a very important and powerful unwritten rule. Inattention and lack of homework when dealing with customers rarely goes unnoticed, and is invariably a costly error.

Lack of proper understanding of the rules (when to follow them, and when to make exceptions,) can lead to higher risks. With increasing complexity in the world, the rules constantly change and proliferate. One of the rules we tend to believe is, "If it's not broken, don't fix it." In other words, if it works, leave it alone. Followed blindly, we will continue to use equipment until it breaks. In many cases, once broken, it may not be possible to repair, and we must instead buy a new one. Would you like to be on a plane that has maintenance done according to this rule? Furthermore, a replacement may not be feasible. It is therefore important for us to know when to apply rules and when to make an exception. Lack of understanding here creates higher risks for multiple stakeholders.

Understanding cause and effect Our curiosity drives us to understand the how and why of things, it leads us to investigate cause and effect relationships between the events. We believe that by doing so, we can predict outcomes, discover truth, and have a sense of control.

Unfortunately, true knowledge of cause and effect relationships is hard to get, and is becoming more difficult because of the growing complexities in just about everything. Products, services, and businesses have become a web with numerous connecting nodes. One thing that goes wrong at a distant node can easily send shock waves reverberating throughout whole organizations, and even countries. For the same cause, one effect can be positive, and another can be negative. Further, these can be separated by time; the positive effect may be felt short term, the negative follows in the longer term.

Complicating matters further is the increasing reliance on data. Data analysis therefore needs to be understood well, and conducted properly. When this ability is missing, or deficient, the Signal to Noise ratio can be poor, and the results catastrophic. Then there is the question of discipline and courage to make the right decisions when analysis and signals call for action. Missing the opportunity to act at the right time is just as bad as faulty analysis.

Hurricane Katrina offers a prime example. Computer models predicted the scale of damage it could cause. Forecasters issued alerts about the ferocity of the hurricane, yet the efforts to save the city of New Orleans, and other communities were minimal at best. Here are more examples.

In the past, companies from leading western countries used the consumption of beverages, or carbonated soft drinks (cause) as a measure of quality of life (effect) to lure lesser-developed countries to adopting their use. Now, we see efforts to remove soft drink dispensing machines from school campuses in the west. Why? High beverage consumption contributes to bulging waists and creates other health problems in the longer term.

Was this risk unpredictable in light of the fact that a typical beverage contains over 25 grams of sugar, and that the lifestyle of teens was becoming more sedate? However, habits once formed are hard to break. Time will tell how long it takes to change a soda-addicted nation.

3. Complexity in Products and Services

We see the benefits of our progress everywhere, however, we have some people drowning in affluence, while others live in abject poverty. We no longer worry about diseases like the plague, but view obesity as the new disease. Products and services available today have reduced the need for several activities we used to perform just a generation ago.

Many of these products and services have indeed proven to be a boon to mankind, but at the same time, a significant number have made us dependent on them for our survival. When they fail, we find ourselves unprepared for the consequences. Entire cities and social structures have become built around the automobile, for example, which in turn is critically dependent on gas or oil.

What happens when the level of complexity is greater than one can handle? Take the example of programming an ordinary VCR or DVD player. So formidable a task for many, that they never take the time to set the clocks on their units, and the poor thing spends its life blinking 12:00...blink...12:00... blink... 12:00.

Then we have the BMW 745i. As *Road and Track*[6] put it, "If you want to change to a radio station that's not one of your presets, here's what you must do. Tug the controller back, rotate it clockwise two clicks, depress it, rotate it clockwise two more clicks, depress it again and then, finally, rotate the knob to your desired station."

Got it? That makes it six steps, assuming you know the right sequence, all while looking at the display instead of the road ahead. A $70,000 car should make things easy, not distract the driver. BMW expects that the kind of technology the 745i introduces will become more common in the future and that drivers will adapt to it. This attitude brings to mind an outdated philosophy of technology exemplified by the motto of the Chicago Century of Progress Exposition of 1933: "Science finds. Industry applies. Man conforms."

Several more examples exist, from simple consumer products to complex high tech equipment, and medical products; in a majority of the cases, increased complexity is accompanied with higher levels of risk.

4. The Business World Today

Repercussions of complexity and connectivity Not too long ago, the artisan built everything from scratch, made to order, or inventory for anticipated sale. The craftsman knew every detail of the product and everything that went into building a particular product, including parts, processes, and techniques. Doctors knew their patients and their families. Barbers knew their customers by name, and their preferences.

Money was exchanged between the buyers of the product and the vendors, thus creating a direct dialog between the two key stakeholders. Vendors knew their customers, and understanding their customers' needs wasn't that difficult.

Few products were built, and every one of them was unique. However, this made for difficult repairs and replacement. Risks to the buyer and the owner were easy to see and comprehend. Risk in the use of products was visible because the products were simple. The chain of cause and effect was short, narrow, and transparent. Even if the rules were unwritten, it was easy to figure out what they were.

In addition, the craftsman could easily sense the needs of his community and users readily saw how everything was linked and how things worked together. They understood how to harness a horse; where the horse was harnessed; how the pull he exerted moved the carriage; where the axles were; and how they supported the coach; and for the brakes to work all one had to do was pull the leash on the horse. Indeed, this made for a much simpler life.

Then came the Industrial Revolution and life changed drastically. Large volume manufacturing set in. Products at lower prices hit the market and became available to the masses. Increasingly complex products and technologies were born. During the more than one hundred years since the Industrial Revolution, products have grown in such complexity, that few of us have a total understanding of what they are capable of, or how they work. Businesses accordingly have also grown very large and complex.

For most products or services today, no one person can do it all. Specialization has become engrained, a necessary development because of the increase in the level of knowledge, and vast numbers of new disciplines. Several of these disciplines (such as Behavioral Finance, Bio-Mechanics, and Bio-Electricity) were unheard of just a few decades ago. This is true virtually for just about every field of work. While it is a tremendous boost to what we can do with our time and resources today, it has opened the doors to many new types of risks for which we are totally unprepared. As an example, asbestos was used as an insulating and flame retardant material in many applications. However, it was much later that the health risks from the use of asbestos were understood, which eventually led to its ban in several countries.

In large corporations, the owners are now separated from the people who deliver the product or service, and they in turn are

98

separated from the people who interact with the customer. The chain of communication has become increasingly convoluted, and silos (in the form of departments) have been created. Risk to the survival of the business is little understood by those involved at lower levels since they cannot easily see the consequences of their actions as it impacts the business at large.

In those cases where the small business owner grew their business into a large enterprise, the stamp and mindsets of their founders, stuck around for quite some time. As such, the business entity's behavior reflected the owners' preferences. We see this in several cases including Ford, and Apple Computer in the U.S., Ambanis in India, and Rolls Royce in England. I mention this point to emphasize that a company's culture is strongly influenced by the founding fathers' and senior management staff's viewpoints. If they are oriented to taking reckless risks, that thinking will permeate the organization as well, remember Enron?

As mega corporations were born, organizational structures grew even more complex, and spawned the globe. Management created new departments, and job functions that never existed before were put in place. More companies turned to the stock market for investors and capital funds for expansion and operations. This caused the nature of risk to change. The chain of cause and effect became increasingly obscure with rising complexity. The mega corporations responded with tighter controls over their staff in some cases, and in others they delegate control.

The time lag between the cause and effect took on very different proportions. It took a long time for misdeeds in one corner to become known internally, and externally. So was the case between customer dissatisfaction (events happening externally) and the impact to the bottom line (felt internally) of the companies. Complexity has created a quantum change in the nature and extent of risk, and it continues to do so.

The information age and the technology revolution, which has yet to run its course, have changed things yet again. Now increasing connectivity has shortened the time it takes to communicate, while the speed in understanding cause and effect (in many cases) lags woefully behind. Increasing complexity and pace have both left their mark - many things that took human intervention to make happen before, now happen from remote action, and with lightning speed.

Organizations with multiple layers, many of which existed to serve as communication, command, and control conduits between the ranks, have found themselves burdened with expensive bureaucracy. Such structures slowed things down, and added little value. They have had to lay off hundreds of thousands in the west to slim down and become leaner. In the process, these corporations spanned the globe in the search for the right talent at the right price, and outsourcing took root. Physical, land based borders have been transformed to virtual, increasingly porous borders. Information and intellectual property transfer has become a matter of just a few clicks. Imaginative entrepreneurs have created services of all kinds to meet the challenges posed by these changes. Google for example, started with providing search services so users could find the right information quickly. Now the service sector has become a large share of the economy in virtually every country.

Connectivity played a key role in globalization of business, which has created several new risks, while helping contain many risks of the past. One of these risks is the loss of intellectual property, which is fragile to begin with. Other examples are:

- ❖ Earthquake related supply interruptions from chip producers in Taiwan in the 90s, which created shortages that rippled across the U.S.
- ❖ The FDA's shut-down of a flu vaccine producer in the UK prompting appeals from the U.S. government for healthy adults to avoid taking flu shots so the elderly and children would have enough vaccines, and

❖ Numerous recalls of products that originate from China due to contamination, or use of banned ingredients such as lead paint.

These are just some examples of the chain reaction set off due to increased connectivity! Didn't anyone think about our critical dependence on just a few sources for flu vaccines?

Sharpen the thinking process More disturbing, even if you don't commit any of the ten mistakes discussed earlier, trouble can still happen because of the actions of others. This means we cannot afford to drop our guard, as Lance Johnson an ex FDA official commented during an interview, "I have seen companies do very well in compliance matters over a certain period, but keeping it up on a consistent basis is a different story."

He says this applies to small, medium, and Fortune 100 companies as well. Therefore, we must continue to sharpen and broaden our skills in risk management, while keeping them in crisp working order. Much like staying current with the anti-virus software for your computer.

According to a survey cited in the August 26, 2006 issue of *Information Week*, 81 percent of the companies reported lost laptops containing sensitive information. The article also mentioned that most used or discarded hard drives from several sources in Germany, U.S., U.K., and Australia still have sensitive information on them. That includes such things as payroll data, cell phone numbers, IP addresses, bank, and credit card information. This offers a prime example of the new types of risks created from the information age and technology revolution. As of now, it lies, together with scores of others like it, in the blind spot for the vast majority of people.

The bigger question is: How is the human species adapting and learning? Can we stay ahead of the curve given that the amount of change seen within one generation far exceeds the amount of change in the last 2,000 years? The whole notion of obsolescence of knowledge has undergone a change, and the half-life of new knowledge is shrinking at an ever-faster pace. Do we know how to deal with this, or are we doomed to repeat the mistakes of the past? Perhaps a schematic sums it up best – as shown in Figure 10.

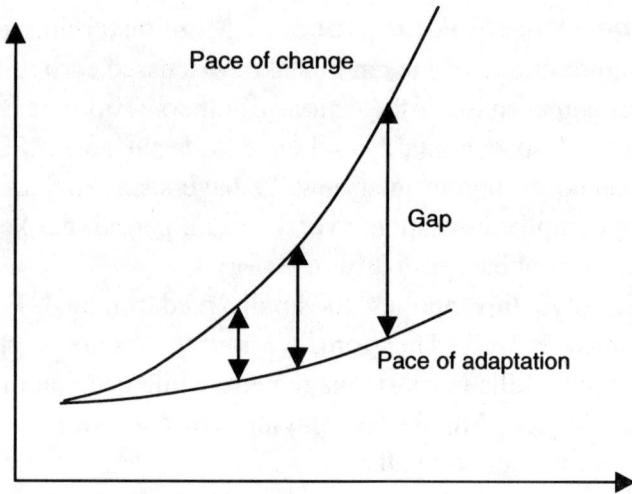

Figure 10. Change vs. Adaptation

For businesses to function in the world today, complexity, and connectivity have become indispensable. These bring new risks in their wake, and the question is *how prepared are we?*

4. Fear and Emotion

Deeply engrossed in a phone call with a colleague, I paced the sidewalk near my office during a hot summer day in 2005. Reaching a shady spot, I paused to escape the sun while continuing my discussion. Suddenly, I experienced a puff of air, and a sharp sting on my head. Instinctively ducking, I found myself under attack from a bird. Thinking the bird had bumped into me while flying, I continued to talk. Then, it happened again.

As I looked at the bird perched on a branch, we made eye contact. He brazenly looked at me and readied himself to attack again, this time head on. Suspecting I had gotten too close to a nest, I quickly moved away, but the bird refused to leave me alone. Relief came only after I had moved about 50 yards from the trees. Later, back in the office I wondered about this quarter pound bird taking on a 160-pound man. Was it survival? Was it fear?

Enron, a company worth $70 billion in capital went bankrupt not too long ago, and it happened rather fast. How could this happen to such a large public company? Enron followed the Darwinian notion of survival of the fittest, putting earnings increasingly ahead of scruples. This resulted in a decision to take advantage of any and every opportunity to make money, whether or not it was legal or ethical. The top people at the corporation were convinced that fraud was merely smart dealing. This lead to a situation where the failure of the company was not an accident waiting to happen, but pleading to happen! Was Enron doing the things it did for survival? Was it fear or was it greed?

When Enron's accounting scandals came to light, along with it surfaced facts about Arthur Anderson, a well-known accounting and consulting firm that worked with them. Kenneth Turan[1], *Los Angeles Times* staff writer wrote in an article, "It was a fraud of such enormous proportions that Arthur Andersen, America's oldest accounting firm, self-protectively shredded a ton of documents dealing with the case before going bankrupt itself."

Emotion and fear rule Extreme emotion and extreme fear both drive people and organizations to do things they would not ordinarily do, even as far as doing things to relieve the immediate emotion and completely ignore the consequences. Subjectivity in thinking increases, and so does the tendency to take reckless risks. The actions of Arthur Anderson could not save the company, neither did they save Enron because these came after the Point of No Return (PONR).

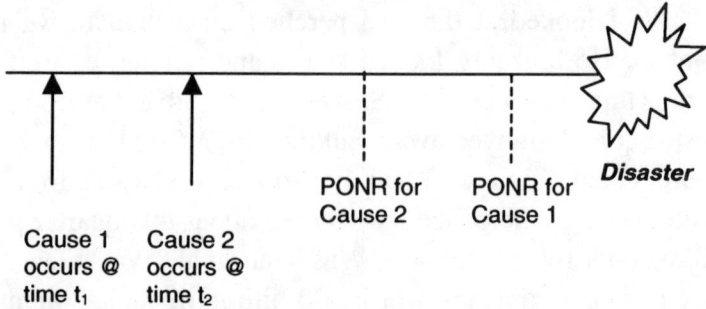

Figure 11. The Point of No Return

In some cases, the time lag between causative events and reaching the stage of extreme reaction is short; in others, it is considerable. When less severe events (or causes) keep occurring over time and accumulate a large number of PONRs, they eventually coalesce. The brain processes the accumulated psychological trauma as a single event of high severity, and we respond accordingly. Material objects exhibit similar phenomena via accumulation of fatigue cracks. Somewhere between the causative moment and failure, there is a tipping point, which once crossed makes failure inevitable. I call this the PONR. Once the PONR is crossed, the only option is to reduce the extent of damage.

In the case of the Columbia, the failure was the inability to withstand re-entry temperatures, and cause was damage to the insulating tile on the leading edge of the wing. The PONR came at that moment when the insulating tile was damaged during takeoff. This point is the PONR because based on design and operation of the system, NASA had nothing in place to stop or prevent failure from occurring after damage to the tiles occurred, or if they did, they did not deploy it. In the case of Enron, several causative factors existed that led to the company's demise. Each factor had its own PONR, and collectively they added up over time, resulting in a bursting of Enron's bubble.

We should understand that each causative event would possibly have a unique PONR as shown in Figure 11.

In summary:

- An understanding of the human element is crucial to risk management.
- We as the human species have a long way to go, in enhancing our ability in this area.
- Extreme emotion causes extreme behavior, one mostly driven by instinct. Such behaviors short-circuit the logical thinking processes and increase risk. This will likely continue to increase unless we unlearn some of the nature-programmed behaviors and replace them with those that are more appropriate.

So let us discuss what can we do. That is the focus of the next chapter.

Sources:
1. http://www.calendarlive.com/movies/turan/cl-et-enron29apr29,0,5674032.story?coll=cl-turan
2. http://dssresources.com/cases/spaceshuttlechallenger/index.html
3. http://history.nasa.gov/Apollo204/
4. http://www.sawstop.com/about.htm
5. http://hubcap.clemson.edu/~campber/piaget.html
6. http://www.alteich.com/tidbits/t010603.htm

Chapter 15

How to Avoid The Ten Mistakes
The Antidotes

The previous chapter makes us realize that human capability in the area of risk management is still nascent. Now we will begin looking at what we can do to improve in this area. This journey begins by briefly exploring six approaches, and continues with a discussion of tools and techniques that address each of the *Ten Mistakes*. When we complete this chapter, we will have a framework and specific actions that are necessary for better risk management.

By far, the first and most important antidote is awareness of the ten mistakes, and understanding how your own personality pre-disposes you towards risk management. Keeping them in perspective *"at all times"* can help prevent the occurrence of such mistakes. Consider this as a vaccine that becomes a part of our thinking system. It will take time and practice to make the vaccine work. Let us begin with the six essentials required to create a framework for managing risk, they are as follows:

1. Strategy for Risk Management – A plan, method, or system to manage risk. A risk management strategy requires that every organization have a method for evaluating and managing risk.

2. Diplomacy – Negotiations and conduct, both internal and external that ensures risk management will be done without the use of coercive measures to the extent feasible.

3. Tactics – Concrete actions and plans that enable the strategy to work, and reduce the levels of risk.

4. Logistics – To position the resources and means for Risk Mitigation after the sources of the risks are identified.

5. Creativity – Out of the box thinking (imagination and ingenuity) that can enable risk avoidance, management, and or elimination. Creativity can also help identify unanticipated risks.

6. Analytics – Quantitative methods to reduce the abstract nature of risk, identify dimensions, and sources of risk, and to study their relationships.

The above actions can be embedded into the operating procedures (framework) for any organization. Then, it is a matter of having the discipline to follow the procedures.

NOTE: Depending on the situation, you may use some or all of the six essentials, and the order may vary.

Next, we will look at how to prevent the ten mistakes. This will be accomplished by first identifying the causes that underlie each mistake, followed by use of tools and/or techniques to prevent such causes. Where appropriate, we will use graphical and computational methods, which enhance our ability to penetrate the fog of uncertainty created by risk. A more rigorous statistical approach falls outside the scope and I will discuss it in a subsequent book. These tools and techniques have delivered powerful results, as has been witnessed in over 100 seminars, workshops, and applications.

Lest we get carried away, I will encourage you to remember that learning is an ongoing effort because the frontiers of risk often recede faster than our advance. Therefore, staying vigilant is important. Toward that end, I recommend you to wear the hat of a perennial student. The downfall starts when we begin thinking: "Now I know all there is to know. I am *the* expert!" So, let us begin with the first mistake, *The Terribility Factor*.

Addressing Mistake 1: The Terribility Factor

This mistake results from the dread of failure or potential failure. The severity of the effects of failure overrides all other considerations, and makes us focus on Terribility alone.

Since the mistake is related to dread, we must understand the extreme emotions that may be at work, and control them. This requires physical as well as mental well being, for which rest, nutrition, exercise, and the right frame of mind are essential pre-requisites. If you find getting into a more rational and thoughtful state is difficult on your own, get help from a trusted friend or associate. Once this state is achieved, we can use the "Severity Rating Scale" as a tool to quantify the impact of risk.

The Severity Rating Scale uses an absolute or relative scale to associate severity with a number. When definitions used in the Severity Rating Scale are clear and unambiguous, it reduces subjectivity in understanding the impact. If it exists, the scale may be used directly or modified to fit the situation. Otherwise, the scale has to be constructed.

Construction of the Severity Rating Scale involves studying what you have experienced so far, and a few other scenarios. To make ratings easier and more objective, create anchor points: one at the most malignant level, one at the least malignant level, and one in the middle. Then compare your situation with these three levels to find an appropriate rating for the current situation or risk.

Here is how to build one. Ask yourself the following questions, and answer using a scale of 1 to 10, with 1 being the lowest magnitude of severity, and 10, the highest.

1. What is the worst risk you have ever *actually* faced? Give it a rating of 7 on a scale of 1 to 10.

2. Imagine the worst risk that *could* come your way. Rate it a 10. (It has to be worse than what you are facing at this time, as well as worse than the one listed in 1.)

3. What is the least risk from things gone wrong you have faced before? Rate it a 1.

Severity Rating	Risk Description
10	Worst imaginable risk
9	
8	
7	Worst risk faced to date
6	
5	
4	Mid level risk (between 1 and 7)
3	
2	
1	Least malignant risks you have known of

Figure 12. Severity Rating Scale

6. What is something you have faced that might deserve a rating of 4, exactly in the middle of the two extremes of 1 and 7?

7. How does the current situation compare to the four anchor points (1,4,7, and 10)? Assign a rating accordingly.

Caution: While these severity ratings may lead you to think that you can use this scale alone to prioritize risks, I ask that you wait for now.

Severity is only one dimension of risk; there are others as well. They are Occurrence and Detection. Ratings in all three are *multiplied* to obtain the Risk Priority Number (RPN). This ensures risk is studied multi-dimensionally, and in a balanced approach.

The severity rating scale is useful in many ways, so think of its construction as a good investment of your time. It will include *some* of the biases of those who constructed it. However, as it is anchored at several points to something more tangible, the biases will be reduced.

As mentioned earlier, extreme emotion and fear increase subjectivity, so it's important to keep these in check when constructing a rating table. Because it may be impossible to eliminate all subjectivity, the use of calibrating questions can help maintain accuracy, and is highly recommended. Failing to do so results in commission of several other mistakes such as: Confidence without Competence, and confusion between Signal and Noise.

The following example is a scale from a company performing fleet maintenance. It was created during an assignment with them in 2004.

Severity Rating	Risk Description	Operational Risks in Fleet Maintenance Workshop
10	Worst imaginable risk	Shop catches fire, and or fatalities occur
9		Repaired vehicles prove dangerous to driver/others
8		Electrical short and or arcing occurs in electrical circuits
7	Worst risk faced to date	Employee trips or slips, falls, and is injured
6		Over budget by >50%, repaired vehicles fail in field again
5	Mid level risk* (between 1 and 10)	Internal accident, causes damage and or delays
4		Non injury collision (regardless of kind) inside shop
3		Shop goes over budget in quarter by up to 10%
2		Delays in carrying out repairs
1	Least malignant risk you have known of	Trucks scrape side during entry or exit

Figure 13. Example Severity Rating Scale

*Mid level risk was rated 5 instead of 4 to comply with an existing procedure within the company

Once the Severity Rating Scale has been constructed, its validity, and understanding can be tested using calibration questions.

Ideally, an independent observer would ask questions as follows:

1. Being over-budget by greater than 50 percent is more severe than an internal accident that causes no damage or delays.
    True or False

2. Repaired vehicles that prove dangerous to the driver and others is more severe than an internal accident that causes damage or delays.
    True or False

3. Being over-budget by more than 50 percent is less severe than repaired vehicles proving dangerous to driver and others.
    True or False

4. The shop catching fire is more severe than repaired vehicles and their potential danger to drivers or others.
    True or False

5. What is worse than the shop catching fire?

The answers to calibration questions can be tallied against the severity ratings from the Example Severity Rating Scale in Figure 13. This ensures the scaling is accurate.

If you use quantitative data to construct any rating scale, be sure to prune the data and remove outliers (Appendix B). This will ensure the integrity of the data before the scale is built.

Severity Rating Scales help quantify one of the dimensions of risk, and control The Terribility Factor.

Addressing Mistake 2: Recency and Frequency

Like a fog, Recency and Frequency restrict our ability to look back and determine causal events. This occurs because recent events are easier to recall, and/or because of the frequency of such events etch them in our memory. Again, the way it affects our perception of risk is by over-riding other factors. Once that happens, our priorities get mixed up, leading to errors when we diagnose causal factors of failure or risk.

Keeping a record, much like a daily diary or Log Book with occurrences of events can go a long way in preventing this mistake. If maintained accurately, these records provide an unmistakable trail of evidence. This can help clarify what caused the risk or failure, rather than depending on memory, *which is unreliable*. The logs can be manual or automatic, and paper based, or electronic. I prefer the automatic log so that we don't have to remember to write things down, similar to the black boxes in airplane cockpits,. Electronic logs in any case are superior since they can enable quick searches and data mining. If the logs are manual, we need to document the facts as close to real time as possible to minimize the effects of time dependent phenomena and changing perceptions.

The down side to automatic logs is that if something worthy of note occurs, the logging system may not be smart enough to recognize and record it. Manual overrides and edits can minimize this lapse. Do not assume that you have to wait for an incident to happen before you analyze risk. Periodic review of the logs can be made as standard practice; doing so increases the chances of early detection of risks, and establishing correlations to better understand cause and effect relationships.

To create an effective Log Book, one needs to determine:

(a) What risks need to be monitored.

(b) The factors that create such risk.

(c) Define their normal operating ranges, and periodicity for recording observations.

The periodicity of logging events will depend on several factors such as availability of personnel, time, working hours, etc., One needs to be aware that cyclical variations can result in overlooking various signals, bias, or distorted logs. An example of records from a fast food franchise chain is shown in Figure 14. One of the company's key concerns was the number of customers waiting in queue, and they monitored the queue length closely using a Log Book at the counter. Numbers within brackets are the normal range of operation in each case.

Date/Time	% Employees Absent (0-5)	% Equipment Down (0-2)	% Material Unavailable (0-3)	# in Queue
3/12/06, 08:15	0	0	10	2
3/12/06, 12:22	10	0	20	3
Comments: Basket ball game in town				
3/13/06, 14:39	9	12	5	0
3/13/06, 22:09	15	0	0	2
Comments: None				

Figure 14. Log Book Records for Customers in Queue (Random Samples)

You can use data from logs to make sensible estimates and analysis. When numerical data is available, creating Statistical Control Charts is an excellent way to detect signals and trends before it is too late. Such charts are constructed from the data collected over a period of time, and help identify the control limits within which we may expect a process, product, or system to perform. There are times when outcomes may never have gone as far as these limits, however based on the data the chart suggests that these extreme values are to be expected. Additionally, indications such as two of three successive observations close to a control limit can provide important clues to when the process is showing signs of *abnormality*. These indications serve as early warnings and improve the chances of detection of causes ahead of the PONR. For more on Statistical Control Charts, please see Appendix A.

Regardless of the type of log, people often fail to maintain them, and they are sometimes seen as a non-value added activity. Few companies document the events in the life of a business unless required to do so by regulations or their customers. Management standards such as the Quality Management System (ISO 9000) require companies to identify and document their processes. However, the logs companies maintain in the process leave a lot to be desired. The Food and Drug Administration requires medical device producers to maintain Design History Files, which is an example of a Log Book documenting key events in the history of a product. Similarly, Control Charts can be used for the same purpose with regard to performance of systems, products, and processes.

Log Books and Control Charts help see through the fog, and minimize the overbearing influence of Recency and Frequency by providing data that can be analyzed.

116

Addressing Mistake 3: Illusion of Control

Primarily because of overconfidence, or our tendency to operate in auto-pilot mode, this mistake leads us to believe things are under control. Often the underlying assumptions are "I" am right, and "I" can control the outcomes. Gita, one of the most revered scriptures of Hinduism tells us, "You have control over your actions, but not over the outcomes." The Illusion of Control can cause untold grief to individuals, businesses, and organizations. We need to remember that even though we may not have control over the outcomes, we still need to have goals, and focused actions to achieve these goals.

Overconfidence is almost like a disease, and more prevalent than most people think. Here are some techniques to save yourself from the Illusion of Control when dealing with people in teams. Pause to consider their capability with respect to the situation or assignment at hand, much like Stephen Covey[6] said, "First seek to understand...." When capability is low, tighter controls and monitoring or feedback loops are needed, but more importantly, without offending those involved. However, capable employees generally need more free space.

For example, say you accept a Project Management position supervising a group of employees on an existing project. One of the first things to understand would be the team's capability, and compare the same with the needs of the project. If employees are new to the company and inexperienced, you will need tighter controls and monitoring. On the other hand, if the team is experienced and highly capable, you may give them their assignments, deadlines, ask them to self-monitor, and report by exception. Imagine how much more you could accomplish if you coached them on the benefits of early intervention, watching for warning signals, and taking early action. In addition, it would bolster their morale to know their boss has confidence in them and encourage them to higher levels of performance.

Role of rewards Often the way rewards are setup is at the root of overconfidence. When this is the case, it is time to re-evaluate what is being rewarded, how it affects behaviors, and, what impact the reward system will have on a short and long term basis. This is easier said than done, since you may be challenging the very system that created the reward structure.

The illusion of control in operation of systems can occur because of the missing feedback loop in the case of open loop systems. The solution is to add monitoring or feedback loops, test and verify to ensure they will work as expected. Case study 7, analyzes a Reactive Gas Delivery System. As part of managing the risk in the operation of this system, a feedback loop was added to ensure the right amount of gases were delivered for processing of semi conductors. Without this, not only would excess gas delivery occur, but it could also have become a safety issue.

For closed loop systems (with feedback), there are two common causes for illusion of control:

1. Inadequate, corrupted or faulty feedback loops, or;
2. Inadequate understanding of system function and dependencies.

The solution for inadequate, corrupted or faulty feedback loops is to test them, correct as necessary, and maintain a state of constant readiness. Ideally, an automatic built-in test can verify their function periodically, alert, and self correct when a fault condition occurs.

To improve understanding of system function and dependencies, System Block Diagrams, and Input Output Maps as shown in Figures 15 and 16 can be used. Once a System Block Diagram has been constructed, identify the outputs for the system, and rank them in the order of importance or criticality.

Suppose in this case the order is O_4, O_2, O_1, and O_3 going from most critical to least critical.

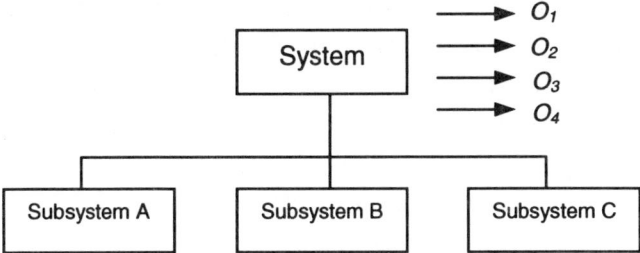

Figure 15. System Block Diagram

The inputs to the system will come from the sub-systems, and not every input will be equally critical to system performance. Mapping inputs to each of the outputs can provide a sense of which inputs are critical. In this case, let us say the mapping of Inputs to Outputs is as shown in Figure 16.

System Inputs (from sub-systems)	System Level Outputs			
	O_1	O_2	O_3	O_4
A_1				X
A_2	X		X	
B_1	X	X		
B_2		X		
B_3			X	
C_1			X	X
C_2	X			X

Figure 16. Input/Output Map

From Figure 16 you can infer that the most important inputs to the system would be one or more from A_1, C_1, and C_2 since they map to O_4, the most critical output for the system. Thus, to ensure O_4 will be within control, we will need to manage A_1, C_1, and C_2. We can apply the same approach to managing risks in projects as well. Just as in systems, projects have deliverables or outputs, and depend on sub projects or tasks for inputs. The Input/Output Map is simple to construct, and is qualitative. A more intensive approach is to use Designed Experiments (a statistical method) to quantify input/output relationships.

The example in Figure 17 shows an Input/Output Map applied to the construction of a recreation hall/auditorium, part of a large construction project. Recent feedback from the Project Manager indicated a cost overrun at the 76th milestone, with 23 more to go. Not wanting to get caught in the Illusion of Control, the Project Manager decided to contain the risk of being over budget quickly.

Hall Elements (Inputs)	Hall Functions (Outputs)			
	Maintain Temp	Safety	Lighting	Access
Floor		X		
Ventilation	X	X		
Heating	X	X		
Air-conditioning	X	X		
Structure		X		
Access Road				X

Figure 17. Input/Output Map for Recreation Hall/Auditorium (Partial)

120

He asked the project team to look at opportunities for cost avoidance, starting with the biggest ticket item in the pending work on the project, the recreation hall.

The team used the Input/Output Map to understand which elements contributed to which function on the hall. Based on this information, they found that the access road *as designed* was quite expensive, compared to the functions it served, and, in relation to the other elements for the hall. The access road was then re-routed making sure there was no impact to any of the key functions for the hall.

You can avoid the Illusion of Control by focusing more on your actions rather than outcomes. When dealing with products, systems, and projects, the System Block Diagram, and the Input Output Map can provide valuable insights. Use of feedback loops is also important in case of systems.

Addressing Mistake 4: The Trap of Comfort Zones

This mistake occurs because of our natural tendency to seek equilibrium, be at ease with our surroundings, and have a sense of predictability. While change is unsettling, we like change as long as we create it, and believe that we are in control. The Trap of Comfort Zones over time can morph into the Illusion of Control.

We can cite many reasons to remain in our comfort zones. Let's take a look at three.

1. Fear of change, or avoidance of pain.
2. Ignorance of what to change to, and how to change.
3. Trapper habits that imprison us.

Fear of Change or Avoidance of Pain The fear of change or the avoidance of pain causes us to stay with what we know, providing us physical and mental comfort. With change comes the concern of leaving behind the familiar, the uncertainty of the new, and a sense of losing control. So we have a choice: wait until the pain of staying put becomes unbearable, or make changes proactively before crossing the PONR.

Ignorance of What to Change to and How to Change

Using two dimensions, the simple matrix in Figure 18 helps you assess where you stand, so that you can take appropriate steps. Here are suggested actions for each quadrant.

		What to change to? (Future state)	
		Know	Don't Know
How to change?	Don't Know	1	2
	Know	3	4

Figure 18. The What and How of Change

Quadrant 1. *The future state is defined, but you don't know how to get there.* Use visualization and event or process maps to go from where you are to where you need to be. Don't do this as a purely mental exercise. Lay it out on a large piece of paper so that an 8½" x 11" sheet doesn't limit you. You may find doing this with a team is more helpful. If you don't have a team, network with professional associations of your industry, a good source to find people who can help. Using a plan backward approach, start from the end state and ask what needs to happen to accomplish this? Continue asking that question at each step moving backwards until you reach the present state.

Quadrant 2. *Both the future state is not defined, and you don't know how to create change.* This will take more effort. First you will need to define the future state. You can do this by studying the direction of industry trends; what your customers are asking for;

and, near term and long-term needs of your organization. Create a vision of what you and your organization need to become. Make sure you benchmark within the industry, or between similar industry sectors to gain a sense of what is already out there. Crossing industry boundaries can also help take blinders off as it did for Southwest Airlines. They studied how to reduce turnaround time at the gate by observing the performance of the racecar pit crews who in 15 seconds change tires, clean windshields, refuel, and service the cars. Once you have defined the future state, you can identify the gaps between the current and future.

Quadrant 3. *You know what to change to, and how to change.* When this is the case, create a project plan to get to the future state, and execute it. During execution, often new challenges begin to surface, so have a will of steel! Make sure your project plan contains meaningful milestones to track progress. Doing *what ifs* on critical milestones in this project plan can put you far ahead in the game by pre-empting potential obstacles.

Quadrant 4. *You don't know what to change to, but know how to make change happen.* When in this situation, the first thing to do is work on what to change to. Failing to do this will result in proceeding on a path with unclear destination. If your goal is discovery and exploration, this may be acceptable. Otherwise, being in this quadrant indicates a lack of vision and leads to wasted time, resources, and effort. See Quadrant 2 for creating a vision.

Note: At times, you may think the future looks hazy. You may have to resort to plan forward, taking a few steps at a time, moving forward, re-evaluating, taking the next few steps, moving forward, and so on.

For those who experience a high level of inertia in getting started, recognize that you may be operating in the high S mode.

Including a high D or I person on your team will create a sense of urgency and result in measurable progress. Recall from Chapter 8, high D individuals are driven, and determined, and high I individuals are convincing and persuasive.

As an example, a Texas company wanted to outsource customer service processes. However, concerns over the new vendor's capabilities, and the customer's potential reactions stalled the company's efforts.

Condition / Horizon	Pros	Cons
No Change	We know the employees Customers know them too. Processes are in place - no new training is needed	Cost structure is high and becoming uncompetitive Customer are beginning to notice this high cost Margins are under pressure due to competition
Change - Near Term Effects	We can inform customers their concerns are being addressed. New customers will be more willing to work with us	Employees in U.S. will be uneasy Training costs of new employees in overseas locations will be high Business processes will need to change Supplier will need to get ISO Cert.
Change - Longer Term Effects	Retain customers, and increase profitability Grow business by being more competitive Add new lines of business	Shut down and sell some local assets Employee morale evaporates Frequent trips overseas Odd hours of work - lot of phone talk time

Figure 19. Pros and Cons of Outsourcing

Their thinking became increasingly clouded as they pondered the possible actions and outcomes. The team was re-organized, and now they included a high D individual. With her help, they studied Pros and Cons as shown in Figure 19. Taking this approach enabled them see things more clearly and take the best course of action for the company.

Trapper habits imprison us The dictionary[1] defines *habit* as "an acquired behavior pattern regularly followed until it has become almost involuntary." Trapper habits develop over a period and can become invisible. Therefore, it is a good idea to have third party neutral observers work with you on critical matters. They can provide feedback on habits that may be trapping you or your organization. This requires them to maintain financial independence, often something easier said than done. Certain behaviors will need to change, and possibly be replaced with others. We will take a brief look at what this involves.

Behavior is the action or reaction we exhibit in response to stimulus, and in relation to the environment. It can be voluntary, or involuntary, and we may or may not be aware of it. It is widely believed that behavior is directly related to the mental maturity or the nervous system, dependent to some extent on circumstances, and the physical well being of the body as well.

When we want to change trapper habits, we must also change behavior. Several factors can help, or defeat attempts at behavior change, namely deep dialog, attitudinal adjustments, personal experiences, intrinsic or extrinsic rewards, and, the will of the individual. An understanding of the preferences and behavioral styles can also provide leverage in re-shaping trapper habits.

Reckless risk is created by *Fire—Aim—Ready* or *Fire—Ready—Aim* types of behaviors, for which the appetite is rather low in the business world. Breaking such trapper habits begins with awareness, and conscious action to offset the behaviors that compromise us. Once you recognize the onset of trapper habits and undesirable behaviors, you can take pro-active steps early.

The trap of comfort zones can be addressed by overcoming the fear of change or avoidance of pain, defining what to change to, and how. Along with this, control of trapper habits is also required.

Addressing Mistake 5: No Time for Risk Analysis

Mixing up of priorities, or not taking the time to set the priorities leads to this mistake. As discussed earlier, some personality types are more prone to this than others. Further, if we have too many things to do, we will need to make smarter choices as to which ones to work on, and which ones to defer.

Today's fast paced, and complex business world can cloud thinking quickly, and when demands come at you faster than you can handle, some things will fall through the cracks. Unfortunately, many who occupy senior positions seem to think of human capacity as infinite. Doubtless, human capacity can grow, however, it has limits.

A two-dimensional approach using Urgency and Consequence makes it easier to prioritize what to work on. This example from an executive team's working session illustrates the method, as shown in Figure 20. In this case, the scores for Urgency and Consequence (numbers 1 to 5) are averages from the executive team after silent and anonymous voting. We multiplied these two to get a sense of the overall importance for each line item, thus minimizing the risk of making a choice based on the Terribility factor, or Recency and Frequency alone. In this case the top three were:

- Prepare for executive summit with customers.
- Review Asia strategy, and,
- Close California facility (not shown in Figure 20).

Executive Staff Prioritization Meeting May 11. For Period: Jun thru Dec 2000 Open Items on Agenda: 12		Scoring Key: 1 = Low 3 = Med 5 = High		
Item No	Topic	Urgency (Date)	Consequence (Overall)	U x C
14	Decide on IPO details with Investment Bankers	2	5	10
15	Complete 5 year strategic plan	2	4	8
16	Finalize mission/vision/values	2	3	6
19	Prepare for Executive summit with customers	5	4	20
20	Review and decide on Asia strategy	3	5	15
21	...			
24	...			
25	...			

Figure 20. Prioritization with Urgency and Consequence

NOTE: In the above analysis, rating of Consequence was not based on a *quantitative* rating scale.

To further address the *no-time* issue we should ask if we can afford to bypass risk analysis. We also need to know the price of a wrong decision, and the chances of making a wrong decision.

Using Cost of Failure, and Probability of Failure, we can quantify the cost of wrong decisions in each case, as shown in Figure 21.

Item No.	Topic	Cost of failure	Prob. of failure	Risk level
14	Decide on IPO details with...	42000	0.2	8400
19	Prepare for executive summit...	88000	0.1	8800
20	Review and decide on Asia strategy	19000	0.4	7600

Figure 21. Using Probabilistic Methods to Quantify Risk

NOTE: The above analysis is based on use of *quantitative* rating scales.

This simple analysis takes the wind out of the argument *No Time for Risk Analysis*. It would serve you well to remember that the high Ds will most likely tend to push things through. To balance that you will need to rely on the strengths from an S type individual. Strong Js will try to bring closure quickly, and you will need to balance that by having some Ps in the team.

No time for risk analysis can be addressed via the use of Prioritization methods that combine Urgency and Consequence, Probabilistic Methods to Quantify Risk, and ensuring a balance in personalities on your team.

Addressing Mistake 6: Confidence Without Competence

We humans lean towards overconfidence. Further, when performance incentives are in place, the propensity for

128

overconfidence is found to increase.[2] This can be a hard situation to overcome because extrinsic rewards drive people to higher accomplishments, while increasing risks from overconfidence.

You can manage this dichotomy by analyzing competence and familiarity, as shown in Figure 22. Make sure the right subject matter experts are involved in the effort (See Weather Forecasters vs. Physicians example in Figure 23.). Think of this as an insurance policy that saves you and your organization from grief.

A software company, embarking on a database project, was in the process of making firm commitments for project dates with their client. During their second meeting with the client, they clarified project requirements, including the purposes and uses for the database. Everyone came to understand that it was to serve as a Learning Content Management System for the company's more than 12,000 employees around the globe.

The vendor's staff, though highly experienced with programming languages and databases in the desktop environment, had not done any projects in this area. The marketing group, thinking that if one knew databases, it didn't matter whether they operated in the desktop environment or on the web, went ahead and made aggressive commits for completion of the project. They had been under pressure because of misses in winning three recent orders, and did not want to miss this one. When the project manager learned of this situation, she had the marketing folks identify which quadrant this project belonged to and had her key staff do the same using a Situation/Competence matrix.

		Competence Level	
		High	Low
Situation	Unfamiliar	1	2
	Familiar	3	4

Figure 22. Situation vs. Competence

The marketing group responded with Quadrant 3. The project staff responded with Quadrant 2. Both were on diametrically opposite sides as far as this project was concerned. There was little chance this project would deliver on the requirements the customer expected. Once this was realized, the project timeline was re-scoped, and additional resources familiar with web database development were brought in. The customer agreed on the re-scoping, however, this may not always be the case. Regardless, one cannot always go by expert opinion, as the next section shows.

Weather Forecasters vs. Physicians – Who is more accurate? Would you believe that weather forecasters can predict weather more accurately than physicians can diagnose pneumonia?

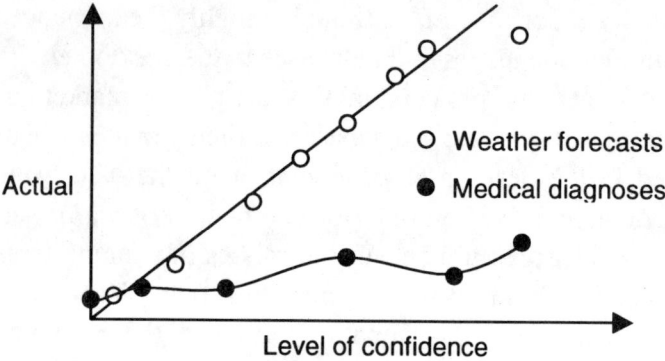

Figure 23. Medical Diagnoses vs. Weather Forecasts
Source: The Psychology of Decision Making and Judgment by Scott Plous
Reproduced with permission from McGraw Hill

Figure 23 shows the extent of error from both.[3] Clearly, being a subject matter expert has its advantages, but does not guarantee accurate decisions. When accuracy is questionable, repeated feedback and practice can make a big difference. Additionally, periodic calibration and checks are necessary to detect and prevent drift.

Calibration checks involve verifying what the experts claim against truth (assuming truth is knowable). When truth cannot be determined, multiple experts are be needed to prevent blind spots from occurring. Further, getting their input independently can avoid the phenomena of groupthink from skewing their inputs.

A fast moving high D individual who has experienced recent successes can easily fall into Confidence without Competence. The antidote in this case is to balance the high D personality with strengths of an S person.

Strong J individuals may be prone to such errors as well due to their preference to make rather quick decisions. When this likely to be the case, including a P, although a challenging move, is a good solution.

Confidence without Competence can be addressed via studying how familiar the task is compared to the available competencies. Further, one needs to ensure that the know-how of the experts is also subject to scrutiny and calibration. Being aware of personalities and behavioral styles will also help minimize this mistake.

Addressing Mistake 7:
Ignoring the Time and Space Dimension

This mistake can occur from not using the right tools to understand cause and effect, or from the incorrect use of such analysis tools. I have identified the Cause and Effect Diagram in Chapter 10, and pointed out the inadequacy of the same. Another tool that is often used is Process (or Event) Map. The Process Map illustrates the steps of a process, in a logical sequence; however, invariably it is constructed with disregard to time and space. Figure 24 shows a typical Process Map with four steps. Notice how one cannot determine the time elapsed between steps, nor where the steps occurred. For example, did step 30 occur in the Packaging Department? What about step 10? No information is available about the nature of the steps either. What was the time elapsed between steps 10 and 20, and between steps 10 and 40? This cannot be ascertained either.

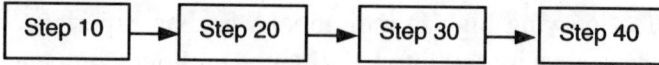

Figure 24. Simple Process Map

Instead of such maps, I recommend creating a multi function map with channels for each function, and time on the horizontal axis. The activities must be aligned in the right sequence, and placed in the right channel. You will need to guard against errors of omission, and those of logic in the construction of these maps.

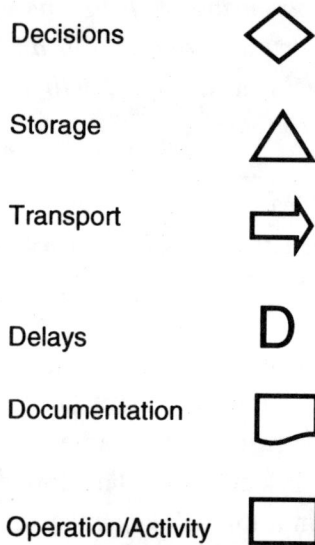

Figure 25. Symbols for Process and Event Maps

When Process or Event Maps are constructed with the right symbols and sequence, they relieve us from taxing our memory with events, their chronology, and dependencies. Displaying these on a large (wall) piece of paper improves clarity. Your maps should answer the 5Ws and 1H (Why, What, When, Where, Who, and How) as much as possible. Therein lies the power of the information that surfaces from a multi-function Process Map.

Considerations in construction of Event or Process Maps:

1. You can build the maps going forward, starting from an initial event and proceeding to the final event, or backward, starting from the end event and proceeding to the first.
2. Construct the map as a team effort for more complete knowledge capture.
3. Whenever feasible, build the maps to reflect the true state of the process. Doing so improves accuracy and shows what really happened. It's one thing to build a map showing how things should be, rather than how things really are. Both serve different purposes

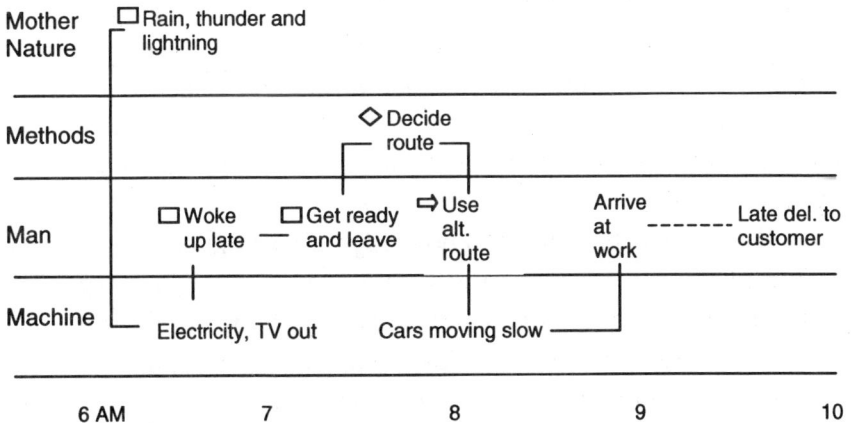

Figure 26. Event Map on Deliveries to Customers on Time Scale

4. Stay away from ink overload. As Dr. Tufte suggests in his books on Visual Display of Data, we need to watch the ink to information ratio. Clutter doesn't help, even if it makes graphics look pretty. As an example, investigation of the Late Deliveries using Process/Event maps is shown in Figure 26.

Ignoring the Time and Space Dimension can be avoided via using the right tools; Process or Event Map as the case may be. Building multi-function maps with symbols, and a timeline on the x axis provide better visibility of the process.

Addressing Mistake 8: Tip of the Iceberg

The tip of the iceberg mistake happens due to lack of due diligence, or lack of knowledge of how to look under the water line. In either case, the result is accepting what is easily visible/obvious at face value. Fact is, most often trouble lurks below surface.

For lack of due diligence, one must ask if this was intentional or un-intentional. If intentional, the responsible parties need to be held accountable for their action. Otherwise, one has to dig deeper to determine the underlying causes and address the same. Now, we may come across reasons such as lack of resources, or funds, etc., matters that are systemic in nature. These are the responsibility of those people who manage the system, including Process Owners, and therefore need to be taken up with them. An example is having a procedure that requires one to look out for icebergs only once every two hours.

To address the lack of knowledge about the causes of risk, a good place to start is historical data if available. The Pareto rule can be applied to identify what is causing the majority of the risk. Doing so separates the vital few from the trivial many. This rule came about from a study of wealth distribution in Italy by Vilfredo Pareto in the early 1900s, who discovered that 80 percent of the wealth was held by 20 percent of the population. Subsequently, this rule is found to have increasingly universal application and appeal; it should be remembered that rule is not an exacting one.

For example, a bank with over 230 locations in the U.S. used Pareto analysis as an antidote against the Tip of the Iceberg. Competition was heating up, and the bank wanted to take proactive steps before loss of customers became a serious issue. It started when a few complaints came to the attention of the Executive Vice President during a surprise field visit. The predominant complaint seemed to be the locations of the branches in Zones 1, 2, and 3.

(1) Zone (Raw Data)	(2) Loss (Raw Data)	(3) Zone	(4) Loss	(5) Cumulative	(6) Percent
1	281	17	793	793	18.8%
2	91	9	705	1498	35.5%
3	107	8	518	2016	47.8%
4	8	19	455	2471	58.6%
5	67	1	281	2752	65.2%
6	86	15	206	2958	70.1%
7	49	12	194	3152	74.7%
8	518	18	132	3284	77.9%
9	705	10	108	3392	80.4%
10	108	3	107	3499	83.0%
11	59	20	102	3601	85.4%
12	194	2	91	3692	87.5%
13	...	...	...	...	...
...	...	...	...	...	...
23	...	...	...	...	...

Figure 27. Pareto Analysis on Customers Lost from 230 Locations

(12 of 23 Zones shown here)

Senior Management took into account the concern voiced by the Strategic Account Teams, and started an investigation. The Customer Retention Team (CRT), an ad hoc group, was tasked with investigating the causes, and make recommendations to increase customer retention. They began by collecting data on gain/loss of customer accounts, and analyzing the same.

To do Pareto Analysis, one gathers the frequency of occurrence (or another variable of interest such as Dollars) and the categories (in this case the Zone) as shown in the first two columns of Figure 27. Then the following steps are taken to complete the analysis.

NOTE: Numbers within parenthesis refer to column numbers from Figure 27.
1. Sort data in the descending order (3,4)
2. Create cumulative totals (5)
3. Calculate percentage for each value of cumulative total (6)

It was clear that 80% of the losses were occurring in 9 of the 23 zones, and Zones 2, and 3 were not in the top 9. Now the question is why the bank was losing customers? Is it location, as suspected earlier, or something else? To answer that question, the CRT probed deeper, this time focusing on categories of complaints/dissatisfaction, and did another Pareto. The results presented in Figure 28 show 80% of the real issues are other than due to Location, as initially suspected. These were hidden below the surface until investigated properly.

The tip of the iceberg can be misleading. To maintain focus on the real causes one needs to exercise due diligence, and build the right knowledge base. When data are available, the use of statistical tools such as the Pareto can help by separating out the few causes that create the most risk.

Customer Service/Experience Area (Category)	% Lost	Cumulative %
Wait time before teller is available	23	23
Time to open a new account	19	42
Time to access locker box	18	60
Time to get a CD made	11	71
Friendliness of staff	9	80
Location/accessibility	8.5	88.5
Wait for business loan approval	3	91.5
Wait for personal loan approval	1	92.5
...	...	...

Figure 28. Percentages by Categories
(Data from 9 Zones, 8 of 15 Categories shown here)

03030S

In the absence of data Let us look at a case when data is not available. One of my colleagues, MR, left the Fortune 100 Company we both used to work for. He had decided to go into business with a couple of partners and called me for a Risk Management coaching session. Having heard of the iceberg concept before, he wanted to look for these as much ahead of time as possible. Being a personal friend I declined any payments for the first three sessions.

We met early in April 2003 to study their operations, and where they were going as a group. The company, JKL Systems (not the real name), was a partnership of three individuals who had never worked together, though they had worked in the same company, and had known each other. They set up their business to provide engineering services in the U.S. (inspection, minor assembly, and simple repairs) for clients with suppliers in far East locations such as China, Taiwan, and Korea.

MR voiced his concerns to me. "I know there are risks out there, but I'm getting so busy, and running around to drum up business, I can barely stop to think and do the *What If's*. So one of these days I suspect we'll crash and sink, which is exactly what I want you to help us avoid."

Perfect! Prepare for trouble before it comes, and when you have the ability to do so. His partners were visiting suppliers in Asia when we started the work of identifying potential future risks.

We started by analyzing JKL's direction, their near-term goals, and their resources. To do this we laid out on wallpaper, a timeline of the significant events and milestones over the next 20 months. I've shown a partial listing of that timeline in Figure 29. Shortly after we initiated this work, all the partners participated.

Major events Apr 2003 to Dec 2004
Date created: Apr 3rd. 2003

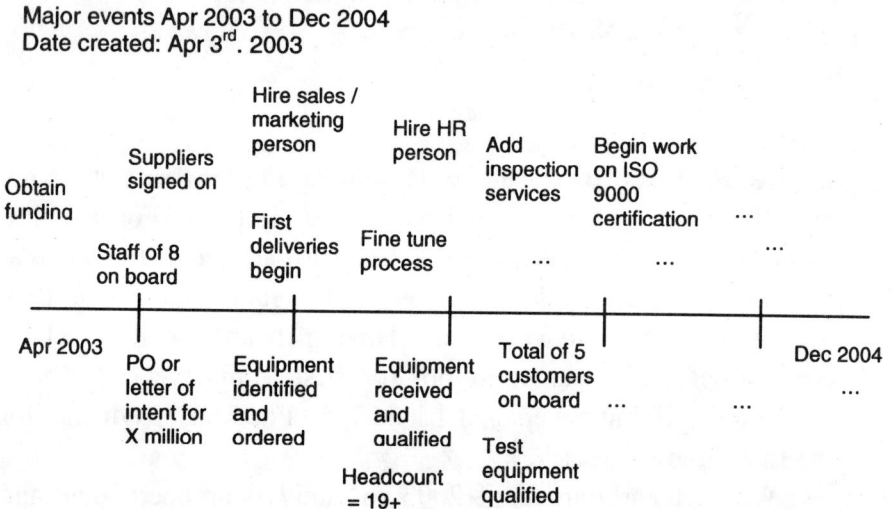

Figure 29. Projected Event Map for JKL Systems

138

This Projected Event Map became a visualization of what they saw their company would achieve going forward. We used three dimensions to evaluate risk: Severity, Occurrence, and Detection. Using this approach, the tips of several icebergs began to emerge. I have listed the top five below with the corresponding RPNs.

Outcome/Event	Risk (RPN)
Deficient cash flow	125
First deliveries unacceptable to customer	100
Employees form a union	100
Not getting ISO Certification by May 2004	75
Enough suppliers do not sign on as promised	75

We analyzed these further to determine the potential causes underlying them. We could not attribute any of the causes to an act of God, and each was a distinct possibility. The company put corrective actions into place for each potential cause before the PONRs occurred. Doing this in the absence of data had its challenges, however, the collective experience of the three partners, and ensuring they stayed away from emotional reactions assured the objectivity of the analysis.

When data is not available, the use of Projected Event Maps to identify the future course of events helps surface risks beforehand. In conjunction with the RPN for each event, the map can be used to locate the PONRs, thus enabling you to put preventive actions in place before failures occur.

Addressing Mistake 9: Confusing Signal and Noise

While this may appear to be identical to the Tip of the Iceberg, it's not exactly the same. Confusing Signal and Noise, or vice versa occurs because of fog, or not having enough know how to separate one from the other. In some cases, malicious intent is the reason for the fog.

There are several reasons why we may mistake one for the other:

* ❖ Not knowing enough about the situation, process, or product.
* ❖ Lack of training and awareness about what to look for.
* ❖ Deliberate attempt at increasing noise level to obscure the signals.
* ❖ Improper measurement systems.
* ❖ Relying on human memory.

The Js, because of their tendency for snap judgments tend to make this mistake more often. To their credit, there are times when a snap judgment is called for and appropriate. Again, awareness of the mistake, and balancing the team with a P personality individual provides the best antidote. The antidote for lack of knowledge is self-explanatory, and implemented by a detailed study of the situation, process, or product. The key is to do it before you cross the PONR.

One could argue that every possibility of what can happen is not foreseeable. While this is true, I'd like to remind you that there is little reason to take reckless risks. Failure to foresee invariably results in more damage. Further, the business world is unforgiving when it comes to taking such risks irrespective of where a business is in its life cycle. We must take calculated risks; they are a prerequisite for success. Calculated risks are needed on an aggressive basis during discovery, and developmental stages of a business.

The antidote for lack of training and awareness in what to look for lies in first understanding more about the situation and then identifying key indicators to monitor. As we identify these indicators, we must define the operational ranges as well. This ensures the signal is triggered for the right reasons.

Next, ensure the signal is triggered with adequate warning so that you can implement preventive action before disaster strikes. You may find that redundant controls are necessary; you are better off knowing this ahead of time, rather than after the failure.

Let's take the example of the leak of hot gases from the rocket motors used in shuttle launches. Upon investigation, NASA discovered that one O-ring might not be adequate to provide a prevent the leakage of hot gases. This could create a serious problem, and engineers added a redundant O-ring. They also studied the gap in the first O-ring and determined that it would lead to excessive amount of blow by, a level that the redundant O-ring would not be able to withstand.[7] This is the kind of thought process and analysis one has to pursue. You must study potential failures and pre-empt disasters.

You may encounter situations where someone deliberately attempts to increase noise levels (or create false signals) to cause confusion, a method whereby one party tries to gain advantage. If you think this can't happen to you, think again.

OK Polymers (not their real name) filed for a series of patents on curing certain polymers, knowing full well that the curing process would lead to poor yields, only about 65 percent. However, they kept the actual process a trade secret, one that produced yields of over 98 percent and was never patented. When OK came out with the polymer they were first to market, and kept the prices high, at $0.80/pound.

Copy cat competitors routinely monitored patent, and publications activities, and three of them fell for the trap. Thinking this was the way to go, they found a way to bypass OK's patents, and entered the field, making significant capital investments. They had found they could make money with prices at $.75/pound.

A few months later, OK cut prices drastically because they could afford it, and still be profitable. In less than a year, each of the three competitors had to retreat with heavy losses.

The antidote is to do *What Ifs* and begin identifying weak spots in your armor. Following this, imagination and taking determined action are a must to prevent failures. The 9/11 attack in the U.S. is an example where signals were missed.

The human species still has a long way to go in preparing itself against such dangers. Technology will help, but may not provide the ultimate solution. The internal ability of the immune system (of the society) to fight is what needs to change, in much the same way the way the human body can fend off attacks from bacteria and viruses on a daily basis. Weaker immune systems offer an invitation to trouble. It remains to be seen what the ISO Standard on Societal Risk Management, and Security will lead to in this regard.

Improper measurement systems result in the wrong measurements, at the wrong times, can be inaccurate, and imprecise. As was the case with the Alaska Airlines jet that went down in the sea near Los Angeles during 2000. Reports indicated that the tools used to check the jackscrew may have given inaccurate readings that led to borderline parts being deemed acceptable; eventually the jackscrew failed during flight resulting in loss of control of the plane's flaps, and it crashed.[8]

The antidote to improper measurement is ensuring the capability of the measurement system. This includes taking several steps, as described below.

1 Identify, and measure the right factors.
2 Ensure the measurement system has the required resolution (limit of detection).
3 Build consistency in measurement.
4 Calibrate the measurement system to a reference or standard.

Keep track of the measurement system performance to ensure the system does not drift over time.

Human memory is malleable and colored by emotions among

other influences. As such, what we recall as a signal may not be that trustworthy after all. The best antidote is recording or logging of events. This may be done manually, or automatically, and stored on tape, paper, or electronically as suitable. Several high-risk transactions are recorded this way on a routine basis; typical are phone call orders and transactions with your brokerage company. The low cost of storage devices is a great enabler in this regard, however, challenges remain. For example, tracking of vital indicators for health occurs only during doctor visits, or after an individual suffers from a debilitating illness. It would be far advantageous to have a smart system that can track such indicators (blood sugar is one of them) regularly; one would then know the baseline and detect changes early, thereby improving the signal to noise ratio. Imagine the benefits of *customized and preventive* approaches to health care.

To prevent confusing between the Signal and Noise one needs to increase knowledge about the system, identify key indicators and their operating range, ensure the measurement systems are capable, and use logs to reduce memory related errors.

Addressing Mistake 10: Rationalization

Our need for comfort, safety, security, and ability to explain cause and effect lies at the root of Rationalization. While we call it a mistake, rationalization also serves as a tremendous learning tool, without which the human species could not be what it is. Trouble starts when we rationalize away things instead of facing them for what they really are.

Most dictionary definitions of "rational" use words such as logic, reason, sensible, and sound judgment. What one person perceives as rational appears as irrational to another. Consider this example.

Someone tells you, "If a card has a vowel on one side, then it has an even number on the other side." You are given four cards as shown in Figure 30.[4] How many of these at the minimum would you have to turnover to decide if the person is lying?

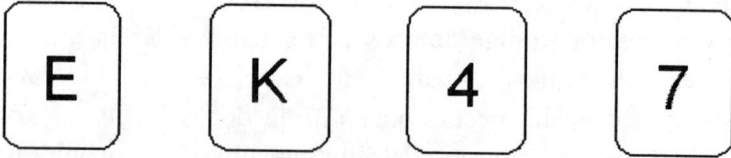

Figure 30. Rationalizing with Cards
Source: The Psychology of Decision Making and Judgment by Scott Plous
Used with permission from McGraw Hill.

Try this with different people you know. Study their responses, and the rationale they offer for their answers.

The extent of reasoning we can put forward often depends on our knowledge about a particular field. However, our beliefs, circumstances, context, and other such factors color our reasoning. Lastly, but most importantly, the extent of automatic processing we are under at any given point dictates how much sound reasoning we put forward. Keeping reasoning sharp is like physical fitness, it requires conscious effort regularly.

The matrix on Truth vs. Rationalization in Figure 31 identifies possible outcomes as a Jury tries to make a decision on Tom; is he guilty, or not guilty? There are four outcomes; two are correct, and two are wrong. No body wants to make a wrong decision, however rationalization *can* lead to incorrect decisions; the results can be devastating as explained on a case-by-case basis.

		Truth	
		Guilty	Not Guilty
Jury rationalizes	Guilty	A	B
	Not Guilty	C	D

Figure 31. Truth vs. Rationalization

Case A, Truth: Tom is guilty
Jury rationalizes: Tom is guilty

Case B, Truth: Tom is not guilty
Jury rationalizes: Tom is guilty
(Can this lead to Tom becoming vengeful?)

Case C, Truth: Tom is guilty
Jury rationalizes: Tom is not guilty
(A criminal walks free; what is the message we are sending to Tom, and to others who know the truth? What is the cost to society?)

Case D, Truth: Tom is not guilty
Jury rationalizes: Tom is not guilty

The antidote is to recognize that we are quite capable of rationalizing the wrong things and make them acceptable or legitimate. Then, use the model shown in Figure 32 to pin point where we are beginning to lose rational thinking.

The model illustrates how we form our knowledge base. From the model, it is clear that the Accept/Reject/Modify screen is where we exercise initial judgment on what to do with the signal. If we decide to accept, it may pass thru the screen unchanged, get modified, or, only selective parts of the input make it through. This can occur automatically without our realization. Whatever passes

145

through the first screen is processed through the filters of our beliefs, values, customs, existing knowledge, etc. and gets conditioned via conscious processing. The conditioned input then goes through a decision step, which results in action, acceptance, or rationalization. Either way a closed loop feedback system works to recalibrate our Accept, Reject, or Modify screen, and internal filters. The model thus describes how learning takes place, becomes part of us, influences thought, and behavior.

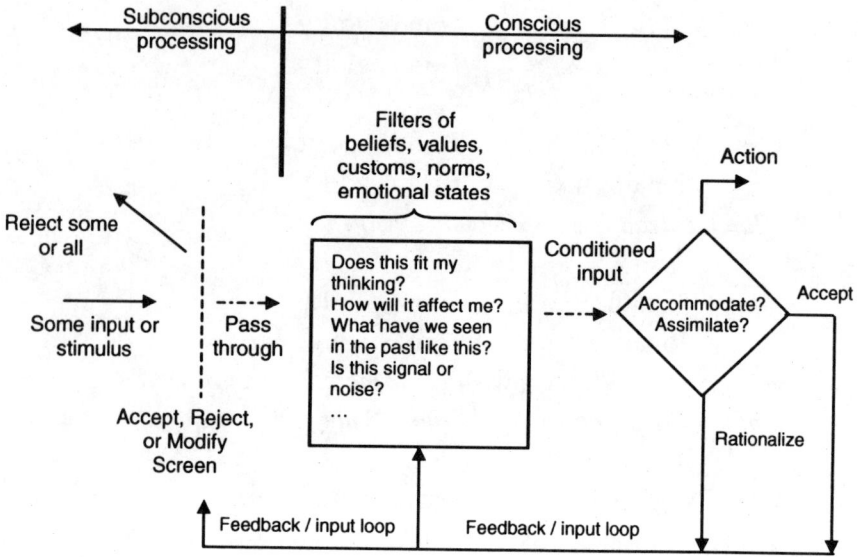

Figure 32. Forming Our Knowledge Base

Example: An employee cautions us about what he saw when observing customers in one of the chain stores that sells our computers. The sales rep spoke ill of one brand while trying to promote another. She found out later that the sales rep did this to earn more in commissions. Implication: they could do the same (speak ill of) to our brand as well.

If we accept the information passing through the first screen, the next stop is conscious processing. As the questions in Figure 32

146

indicate, this is a critical step. Is this a signal, or just noise? Should I believe this employee? Errors made here can have serious consequences since the next step is Accommodating or Assimilating the information. Once opinions form, they become part of our mindset, and over a period of time they get deeply embedded. Thus, done for the right reasons, rationalization can lead to conclusions and beliefs that are more accurate. If done for the wrong reasons, rationalization can cause grave harm. Mindsets can last for decades (as in my case with beliefs about Japanese products) or even generations. It would serve you well to think about where the PONRs are in Figure 32 as you consciously take in information.

> Often the input we receive is from news and media. While they have the right intent of bringing current events to our attention, we should be aware of what is considered newsworthy. Editors[5] look for news values, and the typical order is:
> - Conflict
> - Progress and Disaster
> - Consequence
> - Eminence/Prominence
> - Timeliness and proximity
> - Novelty
> - Human Interest
> - Sex and Romance

To guard against erroneous rationalization enhance your reasoning skills on a continuing basis. To aid in this, you can use the Truth vs Rationalization matrix, and rigorously scrutinize how you form your Knowledge Base, testing it against known truths. A dialog with leading authorities in the field can help tremendously.

Closing Comments on the Antidotes

It must be understood that the Ten Mistakes are by no means the only ones. Further, they can morph from one to the other, and there is no telling which one may occur first.

This chapter presented antidotes to the Ten Mistakes. Although the antidotes were not duplicated between mistakes, you will find that a given antidote works for more than one mistake.

For example, Pareto Analysis was discussed earlier as an antidote to *The Tip of the Iceberg,* however, it is also useful in addressing *Signal to Noise Ratio.* I encourage you to apply the antidotes in creative ways. Doing so will increase your skill in risk management. If some of the antidotes seem trivial, you may be tempted to dismiss them. Don't let their simplicity belie their utility. Now it is time to move forward beyond tackling the Ten Mistakes on an individual basis, and look at a systematic approach.

Sources:
1. www.dictionary.com
2. Scott Plous, *The Psychology of Judgment and Decision Making,* 1993, 221
3. Ibid page 223
4. Ibid page 12
5. Catherine McIntyre, *Writing Effective News Releases,*1992, 27.
6. http://www.quickmba.com/mgmt/7hab/
7. http://pages.stern.nyu.edu/~wstarbuc/mob/challenge.html
8. http://www.historylink.org/essays/output.cfm?file_id=2958

Practice Table for matching the Ten Mistakes to Antidotes

NOTE: The table is for you to fill out, and hone your understanding.

Mistake	The Antidotes							
	Rating Scales	Pareto Analysis	Log Book	Behavior Analysis	⋮	⋮	⋮	⋮
1. Terribility	X	X						
2. Recency & ...			X					
3.								
4.								
5.								
6.								
7.								
8.								
9.								
10.								

Chapter 16

A Systematic Approach

Having studied each of the *Ten Mistakes* and their antidotes individually, let's explore Risk Analysis and Mitigation Protocol (RAMP). RAMP is a systematic method to managing risk in any situation, system, product, process, or organization (also referred to as the object of analysis). Some of you may recognize RAMP as being based on the time-tested approach "Failure Modes and Effects Analysis (FMEA)." RAMP goes beyond the FMEA in rigor and robustness by applying Tops Down and Bottoms Up analysis. Additionally, it includes the PONR, which is critical in studying the timing and effectiveness of controls used to prevent failures from occurring.

The Tops Down approach begins with the object's outputs and looks for causes inside the object, and its inputs. The Bottoms Up approach starts from the inside object, studying what can go wrong at each of the elements. Each approach has its advantages: one examines the object from a macro level, the other from a micro level. Since the Bottoms Up method touches every element in the object, it is more time consuming. Using RAMP provides us the following benefits:

- Surfaces risk and its sources to increase their visibility.
- Reveals the connection between causes and failure modes *including* the time and space dimensions.

151

- Quantifies risk to enable more rational prioritization, and provides a timeline to identify the PONR.
- Determines a rational threshold to provide a benchmark for tolerable risk, and determine if the residual risk after corrective actions is below the threshold levels.

The steps involved in RAMP are provided below, followed by how to carry them out. Both approaches are shown, with the applicable steps for each (see X marks).

Step No.	Description	Applied To	
		Tops Down	Bottoms Up
1	Identify the object of analysis, whether a system, product, process, organization, etc., and its size	X	X
2	Select a team to conduct risk management on the object of analysis.	X	X
3	Define the outputs and inputs for the object	X	X
4	Understand object's functions, and its environment	X	X
5	List the constituents, process steps, or component parts of the object.	X	X
6	Create an event map, process map, or block diagram. For a complex system, you may need to create these at multiple levels.	X	X
7	Convert each output into a failure mode by assuming the output does not meet its requirements.	X	

Step No.	Description	Applied To	
		Tops Down	Bottoms Up
8	Analyze each failure mode and trace the causes.	X	
9	Identify Current Controls (checks and balances) for each cause* that has been identified in step 8.	X	
10	Begin with each event or process step and ask: "What can go wrong here?" The answers will be local failure modes.		X
11	For each of the items in step 10, identify any Current Controls (checks and balances) that may be present.		X
12	Assign ratings for Severity, Occurrence, and Detection for each cause* (or local failure mode) and calculate the Risk Priority Number.	X	X
13	Identify the PONR for each cause* (or local failure mode) starting with those at high RPN. Determine if it will be detected before, or after the PONR.	X	X
14	Use a PONR Modifier to adjust the Risk Priority Number. We will call this the Adjusted RPN.	X	X

* I recommend cause rather than failure mode to make it more pro-active

Step No.	Description	Applied To	
		Tops Down	Bottoms Up
15	Identify a threshold of "Acceptable Risk," and the risks that lie above this threshold.	X	X
16	Identify Corrective Actions and where to apply them in the process or event map, or in the block diagram for the system.	X	X

Introducing PONR in the analysis adds power to the traditional FMEA by evaluating the timing of detection in the chain of events. Now let us understand how to accomplish each step.

Detailed Discussion of Each Step

1. Identify the "Object" of Analysis and Scope

Individuals, companies, and organizations face countless risks, some benign, others malignant. You cannot take the decision of what to work on lightly because time and resources are finite. Hence, first identify the right object of risk analysis. Incorrect selection results in the wrong focus and a disaster that could have been easily avoided. *(Which of the Ten Mistakes could lead to wrong focus?)*

To improve your ability to select the right object, I will share three tools with you: Pair-wise Comparison, the Un-weighted Prioritization Matrix or Pugh Matrix, and the Weighted Prioritization Matrix. These are described in Appendix D. They enable identification of what to work on. You may also find the Pareto approach handy in addressing this matter.

You will also need to scope out the object (is it a nuclear power plant, or a small office building?) to get a sense of the effort required. Then you can decide whether to study a few aspects of the object, or have multiple teams organized to conduct RAMP.

2. Select a Team for Risk Analysis

Because each one of us has a limited field of view and understanding, a team can help prevent blind spots. Too small of a team will not provide adequate coverage, however too large of a team can get bogged down. The ideal number of people is about six or maybe slightly less. If you find you need a larger team, consider breaking up the size of the task so multiple teams can work simultaneously. When analyzing large systems, you may need a higher-level team comprised of the leaders of other teams.

Consider the personality profiles and behavioral preferences of individuals, and the team leads. Maintaining the right mix of personality types is important. This will ensure that the team functions well and does not become a victim of groupthink, or get hijacked by one very vocal member (a high D, or a very vocal J).

3. Define the Inputs and Outputs for the Object

Defining the inputs and outputs of the object allows us to begin identification of known and potential failures that can occur. The easiest way to get started here is by asking questions such as:

❖ What does this object do, and what does it need for that purpose? How are the inputs converted into outputs?
❖ What enters the object and what exits the object?
❖ What is consumed in the process?
❖ What gets transformed?
❖ What comes out?

155

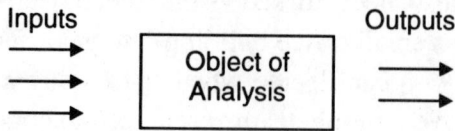

Figure 33. Inputs and Outputs for the Object of Analysis

The inputs and outputs listed here become useful in several of the subsequent steps we will discuss.

4. Understand How the Object Works and the Environment in which it Operates

Understanding how the object converts inputs into outputs elucidates the conversion mechanisms. You can accomplish this step in several ways: by studying, operating or using the object, talking to experts, and researching available user's guides or manuals, and more importantly taking time to understand the science (where applicable) behind the conversion mechanisms.

Studying the object's environment, helps provide a better perspective on potential failure modes and causes. For example, a call center located in a city prone to flooding is likely to have higher absenteeism, affecting response time to customers calls.

5. List the Constituent Parts, Steps, or Events (Elements) that Make the Object Work

Using one sticky note per element is a good way to list all the elements that make the object work. Case study 7 provides an example of how this was done during risk analysis for a Gas Delivery System. The ideal way to obtain this information is first hand. For products, you may look up the prints, and or the bill of materials. For a process or a service, live through it yourself or involve the people who have first hand knowledge.

156

6. Create an Event Map, Process Map or Block Diagram

Event or process maps illustrate the sequence of events of how the object works. Although creating such maps may seem trivial at first, I urge you not to underestimate the benefits they provide. Human memory has capacity limitations; trying to remember all the steps and their sequence is impractical. Seeing how things connect is not easy unless laid out on paper, as suggested here.

The Process Map or Event Map should clearly show how all the elements listed in the previous step relate to each other. Multi-dimensional maps as illustrated earlier in Figure 26, are far superior in this regard. A block diagram for systems is illustrated in Figure 15.

If conducting Bottoms Up analysis, please go to step 10.

7. Convert each Output into a Failure Mode

Use the outputs listed earlier in step 3 as the starting point to identify potential failures or risks. Each output, when not meeting the required performance, can be considered a failure and therefore, a risk. Make sure known and potential failures are included.

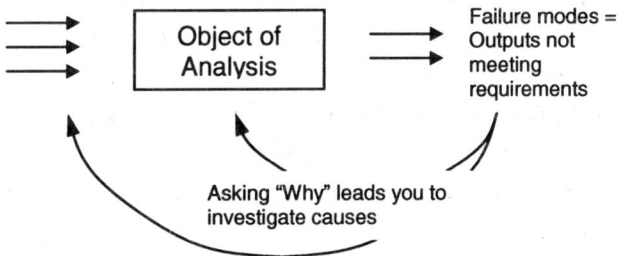

Figure 34. Identifying Failure Modes and Causes

8. Analyze each Failure Mode and Trace the Cause

Ask, "Why and how this failure happened (or could happen)?" This two-part question leads you to identify the reasons behind the failure and whether they lie in process steps, inputs, or events as shown in Figure 34. You will also need the process map, event map, or block diagram as created in step 6. With this map, you can identify all possible causes rather than stopping at what you know, thereby avoiding the *Recency and Frequency* mistake.

9. Identify Existing Checks and Balances for each Cause

Your ability to control and manage the cause of failure has considerable impact on the level of risk. Will the cause get detected, blocked, or trapped? Will it escape and convert into a failure at some point? Causes that can be blocked or trapped carry lower risk levels. Their rating for Detection, and the corresponding RPN values will be lower. You will need to ensure adequate signal to noise ratio for the measurement systems used in the detection of causes.

CAUTION: In my observations and work with dozens of teams performing risk analysis, I have seen them rationalizing and speculating at this point. "Oh, it will get detected (or caught), *we will* have an inspection step here." Such speculation is *not* good practice. You must ask "What *is in place now* to detect or prevent causes from migrating into failures?" If the answer is, "Nothing is in place as of now," then record it as such. This ensures the detection rating will be the highest value, and the RPN will reflect the true risk level.

So far, you have completed the Tops Down analysis. The next steps take you through the Bottoms Up analysis.

10. At each Event or Process Step, ask, "What can go wrong here?"

Analyze each event or process step and ask, "What can go wrong here?" The answers will identify local failure modes which become causes that trigger system level failure modes. Ensure that both–known and potential failure modes are included. This is like taking a fine-toothed comb through the object of analysis, in order to surface known and potential problems. Avoid rationalization of any local failure modes. Unchecked this leads to a false sense of security.

11. Identify Checks, Balances, and Controls for each local Failure Mode (identified in step 10)

For each of the items identified in step 10, study what checks, balances, or controls are present. This enables you to determine whether these local failures will migrate into bigger failures down the road and affect the outputs of the system. (Same logic as in step 9. Also read the Caution for that step).

12. Assign Ratings for Severity, Occurrence, and Detection for each Cause and Calculate the Risk Priority Number

Begin quantification by examining the causes and failures, and by asking several questions.

Ask, "How severe is the consequence of this failure?" to identify the *Severity* rating.

"What are the chances this cause (or local failure mode) can occur?" to identify *Occurrence* rating.

"How good is the control system to detect or prevent the cause (or local failure mode) from occurring?" to define the *Detection* rating.

Use a scale of 1 to 5 or 1 to 10 for each question. Once you decide to use a particular scale, you must stay consistent. After assigning ratings, calculate the product of all three (Severity, Occurrence and Detection) to get the Risk Priority Number (RPN). The higher the number, the higher the risk. Sample rating scales are shown in Appendix C.

13. Identify the Point of No Return for Each Cause

Ideally, you want to know the PONR for each cause. If this is not possible, identify the PONR for at least the causes with high RPNs. Recall that the PONR is that point on the event or process map after which you cannot do anything to prevent the cause from precipitating a failure.

The PONR is as a modifier to the Risk Priority Number. It helps by including the impact of the time dimension, which is often missed or lies buried in conventional FMEAs. Understand that even if current controls are in place, they are useless if the time constant for them to function exceeds the available time before failure occurs. Thus, you can have situations where the current controls are present but of no value.

14. Use a PONR Modifier to Adjust the Risk Priority Number

Using a scale of 1 to 5, or 1 to 10, you can adjust the RPN depending on the location of current controls. When the current control comes after the PONR or the time constant for preventive action is greater than the failure's germination time, use the highest number in the scale. This follows from the fact that despite the current control, we will experience a failure. The number we get now will be called the "Adjusted RPN or A-RPN." The highest value for A-RPN will be 625 (on a scale of 1 to 5), or 10,000 (on a scale of 1 to 10).

15. Identify a Threshold of Acceptable Risk

In this step you define your tolerance for risk. You determine a threshold by studying the causes with lowest and the highest A-RPN values. For example, you may find 129 causal factors exist for a particular object. Suppose the lowest A-RPN is 50, and the highest is 10,000. This step requires you to identify what A-RPN level represents tolerable risk for you. One convenient way to identify your threshold is to start at one extreme A-RPN and work your way down or up to find an acceptable risk level. This risk level must be agreed upon between the stakeholders involved with the object in question. Keep the *Ten Mistakes* in perspective as you make this decision. Pareto analysis of A-RPNs is also used to identify the vital few causes that create the most risk.

Having completed this step, you now have a list of causes that lie above the threshold level and require attention.

16. Identify Corrective Actions and where to apply them

For causes above the threshold, you can begin identifying corrective actions, and place them much earlier than the PONR. New A-RPN values calculated after the Corrective Action should be below the threshold. If they are not, it indicates that your corrective action was not aggressive enough and you must do more to reduce risk.

Conclusion

In conclusion, we have covered the use of RAMP. By now you will have realized it ensures greater robustness in risk management. This comes about from:

- Focusing on what is important (object of analysis).
- Using a team based approach–to minimize blind spots.

- Understanding in detail, what the object does.
- Identifying the known and potential failures.
- Locating the causes of such failures.
- Quantifying risk and linking it to the causes.
- Defining a threshold of acceptable risk level.
- Surfacing those causes that are above the threshold.
- Putting corrective actions/preventive actions in place.
- Re-evaluating risk levels to ensure they are below the threshold.

In the next chapter, I will take you into the future, examining events that have happened in the recent past, and those occurring now. What do they foretell of the risks that lay on the horizon? Think about what these events can possibly morph into. The observations are from the years 2001 through 2006.

Chapter 17

What Lies Ahead?
30 Trends or Events to Watch

In this chapter, we will examine certain events as they unfold. This will be an interesting exercise for you. Study these in the context of the Ten Mistakes of Risk Management and keep a diary going forward on the ones that resonate with you. Perhaps we may exchange notes in a few years, or you can e-mail me your thoughts. These events and observations are for the years 2001 through 2006 and contain the seeds of potentially far-reaching ramifications. Think of the opportunities they present, risks they pose, and to whom.

1. The sale of colas and soft drinks in schools has been discontinued in the U.S., and other countries are considering doing the same. Can this spread all over the world? What will this mean to the multi-billion dollar soft drink industry?

2. China holds over 70% of the world market share in toys. Manufacturing and quality assurance still lags behind the times. Inevitably, this will lead to sub-standard products reaching the market. Who will be impacted and how?

3. Chinese families increasingly host exchange students from the U.S. How will that affect opinions and perceptions about China,

and Chinese products in the U.S.?

4. Singapore is establishing infrastructure to attract biotech businesses. What does this mean to the biotech industry in the U.S., and other European countries?

5. Hospitals and health care service providers from India now actively promote their services to the West. What does this mean to the health care service providers in the West?

6. The growing immigrant population is changing the demographics of the workforce. An increasing number of employees in the West cannot speak English. Will a graying America and Europe be required to learn Vietnamese, Urdu, Arabic, and Spanish in their golden years?

7. Wine and alcoholic drinks will be available online in the U.S. Combine this with an increase in single parent families, and families where both parents work. This means it will be easier for children to order and get such substances without their parents' consent and knowledge. What can happen to substance abuse rates for future generations?

8. Increasing disenchantment among managers and executives with the amount of hand holding needed before outsourcing really delivers the promised savings. Combine that with the frustration experienced by displaced professionals. Will there be a backlash in the West? How far will it go?

9. American universities have been graduating a diminishing number of engineering graduates each year, fewer than 100,000. Whereas, those in China and India exceed 2.5 million. With the opening of those countries' economies, local opportunities for these engineers are being created. Combined with a complex and

bureaucratic U.S. immigration policy, migrating to the U.S. is a less attractive option. How will this impact the growing skill shortage of technical personnel in the U.S. going forward? Currently, the unemployment rate for technical personnel in the U.S. is around 1%. [1]

10. The retirement of over one hundred million baby boomers in the West. What challenges and opportunities will these hundreds of billions of dollars worth of purchasing power create?

11. Aging populations in Japan, U.S., and other affluent countries with low birth rates will need increasing assistance for daily living. Is Honda up to something with their ASIMO robots?

12. The ongoing march of technology promises all sorts of new discoveries and inventions, such as cloning and genetic engineering. Much like nuclear fission, these new technologies can prove a tremendous boost to mankind's progress, and at the same time pose unfathomable risks. What risks will surface? More importantly, what should we doing before a PONR is passed?

13. Under pressure to cut costs of operations, many companies have outsourced business processes to Asian countries. The call centers there take care of processing orders by phone, including credit card transactions, and in the process, obtain sensitive customer information. Many of these countries, such as India, Pakistan, the Philippines, and Thailand, have a dismal record with regard to corruption.[2] What risks does this pose to you as a consumer?

14. Airline companies in India are some of the biggest buyers of commercial aircraft. Many of them are setting sights increasingly on the U.S. and EU markets, and coming up with novel ways to provide entertainment at 35,000 feet. What challenges does this

pose to the airline industry in the West?

15. Undergraduate students grow increasingly tired and frustrated of poor treatment and indifference from professors. At the same time, business and government leaders wonder about the deterioration of education in the U.S. and why it lags behind developing countries in the number of science and engineering graduates. How long before real educational reforms are put in place? Has the U.S. crossed the PONR?

16. Non Government Organizations are doing more to eradicate human misery than many governments despite being short on formal power, authority, and funds. What does this foretell about public confidence in their governments and politicians? Could the leaders of the NGOs gain enough trust from people to start holding more public office positions?

17. The Internet continues to level the playing field by making more information universally available and faster. How will the less connected fill the gap? If the gap continues to widen, will those people increasingly resort to terrorism (or anti-social means) as a way to get even?

18. Ethanol demand in the U.S. is likely to skyrocket due to the focus on reducing oil imports. What does that mean for prices of food grains, and feed for livestock? If this also happens in other developing countries, how will the common man there cope with rising food prices?

19. Google continues its un-relented expansion. What/where is the PONR before it becomes an unwieldy giant (if at all) that crushes under its own weight? I am not against Google – just know enough that few corporations can sustain such growth forever. In the case of Ford – extinction seems to be a distinct possibility after having

been one of the largest corporations on the planet.

20. The world continues to dump greenhouse gases into the atmosphere, and some countries are given exemption from controls on how much they can dump. Have we crossed the PONR on global warming? What if, in truth global warming is not due to man made causes? What does that do to competitiveness of western business?

21. Will we see the extinction of the tiger in the wild in India over the next three decades? What is the PONR for the threshold level of tiger population?

22. China may be the most populous country at this time, however India's fertility rate is higher and will overtake China in population in the foreseeable future. What does that mean to the power balance in the continent? How should the West position itself with respect to the two countries?

23. Lack of local workforce in many E.U. countries is causing them to allow influx of foreigners of different ethnicity who do not assimilate into society. Many of them lead secluded lives, and feel isolated. What is the PONR for a communal violence flashpoint?

24. Many governments in the world recognize the growing problem of obesity, and it is not limited to the West. How long before insurance companies and employers begin discriminating against obese employees and charge extra premium for health insurance?

25. Hundreds of languages have been lost with more on the way to extinction. With that, much of the knowledge of the ages will be gone. What will be the impact and will we ever know?

26. Porous borders between several countries allow people to migrate, often illegally. This creates a great strain and risk on the host countries. U.S., India, and several countries in the middle east experience this. How long can this continue? Is anybody monitoring the PONR before a tipping point is reached resulting in a backlash.

27. A wave of alternative energy solutions is in the making, especially in the Europe and the U.S. That day is in sight when oil imports from the middle east will begin tapering off. How will the countries of that region cope with a world less dependent on their oil?

28. Robotic surgery is taking root, and more procedures are likely to be performed using this approach in the future. What impact will this have on costs of such procedures, and which companies will be the winners/losers in the game?

29. New markets exceeding the size of U.S., and E.U. will be born in India and China; what companies are positioning themselves to avail of this opportunity, and how? Where are they located?

30. In many developing countries there are controls on who can practice medicine, however associated services such as pathology labs have little to no controls in place. What opportunities and risks does this present, and to whom?

Victors manage risk
Victims get managed by risk

Sources:
1. *Investors Business Daily,* September 5, 2006.
2. http://www.transparency.org/publications/annual_report.

Appendix A

Statistical Process Control Charts

Dr. Walter Shewhart at Western Electric started using SPC charts in the 1920s to monitor and control manufacturing processes. The charts were based on data collected from a process or product, and studied to determine if things were under statistical control. We continue to use these charts today to evaluate product and process performance, however, few have used them for analyzing risk.

Every control chart has four elements: Data, Centerline (or the Mean), an Upper Control Limit (UCL), and a Lower Control Limit (LCL).

The UCL and LCL are placed 3 Standard Deviations from the Mean, and represent the limits within which you can expect the process (or product) to perform. Incidents such as data points outside of control limits, and trends—that is, movement upward, downward, sideways, and so on, are indicative of non-random or special causes. These situations imply the process is out of control, and it needs attention. When used with live data, timely intervention prevents a product, system, or process from a severe failure.

Several types of control charts exist and each has a purpose. Three common types are:

- **Variables control charts**: used to track variables such as inventory levels, temperature, rainfall, air speed, etc. Here you can plot individual values, or averages for groups. These charts are known as Individuals Charts, or Averages Charts.

Companion to these are charts that track changes from one data point to the next, or from one group to the next. We call such charts Moving Range, or Range Charts. These help identify significant and abrupt changes.

- **Defects or incidents control charts:** used to monitor incidents, or non-conformances such as defects per car, or number of close calls at airports per week.

- **Percent defective control charts:** used to provide a perspective of how the entire process is performing, using percentages.

Individual Values – Distance Traveled This chart tracks the distance traveled by rockets. Using it, you can study the variation in distance with every launch.

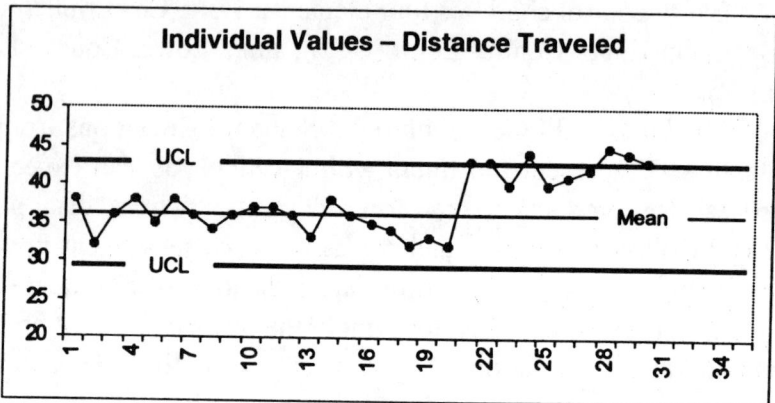

Figure 35. Variation in Distance Traveled by Rockets

In this case, we see a shift in the performance of rockets starting with launch 21. Figure 36 shows *change* in distance traveled from one launch to the next one.

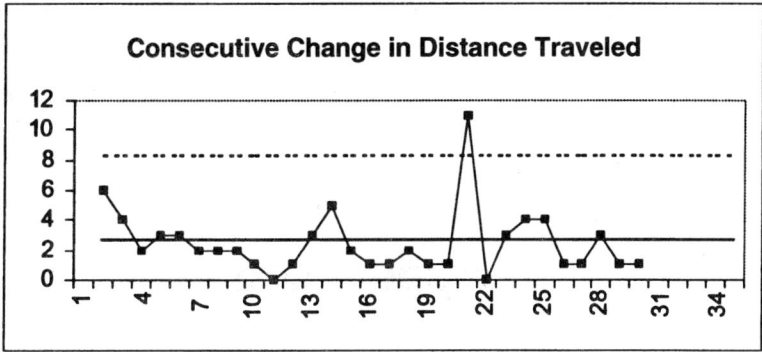

Figure 36. Consecutive Changes in Distance Traveled by a Rocket

Together these charts tell us a story. If the rocket motors begin to show drift in performance over time, or from one launch to the next, these charts can effectively track and alert us to such changes. Figure 35 shows that a shift has occurred, and the rockets are traveling larger distances after the 21st launch. Figure 36 shows that the variability in distance traveled has not changed appreciably, but an incident occurred at launch 21. How would this be relevant in real life?

Imagine this information is not available and rockets are supplied to the army. They continue to use the previous elevation angle settings for rocket launches. All of a sudden, instead of hitting military targets, the rockets now land in civilian areas. This creates a double whammy!

When used properly, such control charts are very effective in managing risk before things get out of hand.

Which of the Ten Mistakes is avoided
by the use of Control Charts?

Appendix B

Test for Outliers

Outliers are data points that are possibly so far out from a given data set as to be considered highly unusual. Therefore, these deserve further probing to determine if they truly belong in the data set or they are due to some kind of error.

Town A	Town B
11	12
16	15
12	16
16	9
9	11
11	19
14	17
21	21
13	11
17	14
15	16
19	31

Figure 37. Toxin Levels in Water Supply (Hypothetical)

Consider the data provided in Figure 37. Compare the Averages, and the Standard Deviations for the two data sets and study the differences.

For Town A: Average = 14.5   Std. Dev. = 3.5
For Town B: Average = 16.0   Std. Dev. = 5.9

Now, suppose the threshold is 15mg/lit. on average. The analysis from the data suggests water supply from Town A is safe, and that from Town B is not. Can you imagine the anguish it can cause to the city officials, especially if the information makes headlines?

Outliers can be on the high side, or the low side. They are also known as Upper and Lower outliers.

The Upper Outlier is defined as any value higher than $Q_3 + 1.5x$ IQR.

The Lower Outlier is defined as any value less than $Q_1 - 1.5x$ IQR

IQR is the Inter Quartile Range – given as $Q_3 - Q_1$
Q_1 is the 1st Quartile and Q_3 is the 3rd Quartile

It would serve you well to verify that data from Town A does not have an outlier, but that from Town B does--the high value of 31. What if investigation revealed that the high value of 31 was a typo? It was really meant to be 13.

Finally, one cannot overlook the importance of due diligence in data collection. In too many cases this task gets scant attention.

If you do not question outliers, and the truth lays buried, which of the Ten Mistakes will this lead to?

Appendix C

Sample Rating Scales

Risk should be studied using three (or more) *independent* dimensions – Severity, Occurrence, and Detection. By rating each dimension separately, and combining them, we reduce the potential to get carried away by any one of them. For example:

- ❖ *The Terribility Factor* forces you to focus *only on Severity*.
- ❖ *Recency and Frequency* drives you to focus *only on Occurrence*.

Using multiple dimensions provides for a more balanced approach to risk analysis. Furthermore, an Adjustment Factor is added that accounts for the timing of the detection and the time constant for the corrective or preventive action to take effect.

Rating scales play a vital role in quantifying the dimensions of risk. Where pertinent data (such as frequency of occurrence) are available, it can be incorporated in the construction and use of rating scales. The principle behind constructing rating scales is simple and is illustrated as follows:

Severity Scale
Low   High
1  5 or 10
Occurrence Scale
Low   High
1  5 or 10

Detection Scale

Easy (to detect)   Impossible

1  5 or 10

- **Severity Rating (for the Effect of Failure)***
    1. Minor inconvenience in personal/work life
    2. Noticeable impact to work schedule/personal plans
    3. Affects relationship with boss/family members
    4. Loss of revenue, relationships, and or reputation
    5. Could cause injury/other safety issues

- **Probability of Occurrence (of Cause or Failure)****
    1. Very rare - maybe once in 10 yrs., or <1 ppb
    2. Rare - maybe once in 5 yrs., or up to 100 ppb
    3. Frequent - could occur more than once /2 yrs., or up to 100 ppm
    4. Very frequent – could occur 1 to 3 times/year or between 100 and 1000 ppm
    5. Certain - more than one occurrence per quarter, or above 1000 ppm

- **Detection Rating (for Cause or Failure)***
    1. Failure or its cause is readily or self evident
    2. Manual inspection or test can easily detect impending failure/cause
    3. Failure is hard to detect, special instruments or training required.
    4. Failure detection will destroy the unit
    5. Failure can slip by unnoticed, and will get detected after occurrence

*The rating scales for Severity and Detection as shown here are qualitative – a rating of 4 for example, cannot be interpreted as being double a rating of 2.
**The rating scale for Occurrence is quantitative; it can be linear or non-linear.

When constructing rating scales for the first time, a 1 to 5 scale is a convenient starting point. This is because a 1 to 10 scale can be somewhat challenging to construct for beginners.

175

Furthermore, rating scales can be constructed on a qualitative or a quantitative basis. A quantitative scale ties the ratings to something that is unambiguously measurable or definable. The trade-off is that the scale tends to be narrow, and may require re-definition when situations change. Qualitative scales *must* be based on clear operating definitions, for example, a Detection rating of 1 indicates Failure or its cause is readily or self-evident. When this Detection scale was applied to studying failures on personal digital assistant devices (PDAs) the definition read as follows: "The PDA beeps periodically, and the battery symbol blinks on the display."

The Adjustment factor can use similar scales as the one for Severity, Occurrence, and Detection, namely 1 to 5, or 1 to 10. The rationale behind this factor is that an earlier warning flag allows us more time to take corrective action or evasive measures. This plays a major role in failure avoidance. The schematic for this scale is as shown below:

Adjustment Factor Scale

Detection occurs early   After PONR
and time constant for
corrective/preventive action is small

1   ———————————————————▶   5 or 10

Of course, early is relative and dependent on the time required for preventive or corrective action. Here is an example.

You are driving on the highway, and a truck is ahead of you. Suddenly you see gravel and rocks falling off the truck (cause). These can hit your windshield, damaging it and impairing visibility (failure*), which can result in a collision or injury (effect).

*Providing clear visibility is a basic function of a vehicle. Therefore, impaired visibility is a failure.

If you were alert, driving at a safe speed, and following the truck at a safe distance, you would have enough time to take evasive action (Detection occurs early with adequate time to take preventive action, adjustment factor = 1).

However, if you were too close and driving fast, even if you were alert, and took evasive action – rocks would hit your windshield (detection occurs, however the time for evasive action is too short, you have crossed the PONR, adjustment factor = 5). Here is a sample of the rating scale for Adjustment Factor based on the time available for evasive or corrective action before the PONR occurs.

Adjustment Factor Rating*

1. Detection occurs early and the time available for evasive action (Time Constant) is 5x or greater than the time to PONR
2. Time constant is 3 to 4x the time to PONR
3. Time constant is 2 to 3x the time to PONR
4. Time constant is 1 to 2x the time to PONR
5. Time constant is <1x the time to PONR

*The rating scales shown here can be modified to suit your purpose; it is not feasible to have one scale work for every situation.

Which of the Ten Mistakes would occur in the absence of rating scales for Severity, Occurrence, and Detection?

Which of the Ten Mistakes would occur if we ignored the Adjustment Factor?

Appendix D

Prioritization Methods

This appendix provides three techniques for prioritization. These methods are useful when prioritizing what to work on, based on relative or criteria based comparisons.

Pair-wise Comparison

Pair-wise Comparison is used to prioritize choices relative to each other. For example, you may have four alternatives, which you need to rank in order of relative importance. Figure 38

	Region A	Region B	Region C	Region D
Region A	X	X	X	X
Region B	Region A	X	X	X
Region C	Region C	Region C	X	X
Region D	Region D	Region B	Region C	X

Figure 38. Pair-wise Comparison Matrix

provides an example from a software services provider with customers in four regions.

The X within any cell indicates where no comparisons are made to prevent redundancy and errors. In the other cells, you make comparisons between pairs. Thus, when comparing Region C against Region A, you ask which is more important? In this case, the answer is Region C. For each cell, repeat the question on a pair-wise basis, and complete the table.

Region	Frequency
A	1
B	1
C	3
D	1

Figure 39. Frequency tallied by Region

Then, a frequency count provides the ranking as shown in Figure 39. The results indicate that Region C has the highest frequency and therefore is the most important.

Un-weighted Prioritization Matrix using Criteria

Un-weighted prioritization matrices serve the same comparison purpose as pair-wise matrices, although the approach is slightly different, see Figure 40. As before you will prioritize between four regions, however, in this case, some criteria exist and you use those as a reference—assuming each criterion is of equal weight. Moreover, you use one region as a baseline.

For this example, West Coast is the baseline, and therefore the rating for each criterion is set to O for this region. Each of the remaining cells is assigned a symbol from a choice of three. The choices are + (meaning better than baseline), O (same as baseline), or − (worse than baseline). Finally, column totals are made for each symbol.

179

	East Coast	West Coast	North	South
Manpower	+	O	-	+
Criticality of Clients	+	O	-	O
Cash flow	-	O	-	O
Market Size	-	O	+	-
Accessibility	-	O	-	-
Total: +	*2*	*0*	*1*	*1*
Total: O	*0*	*5*	*0*	*2*
Total: -	*3*	*0*	*4*	*2*

Figure 40. Un-weighted Prioritization Matrix

Figure 40 suggests that North is worse than the other regions because it has the highest frequency of minuses. Therefore, this should become the first area or object for Risk Analysis.

Weighted Prioritization Matrix using Criteria

This is an indispensable method when you need to decide between alternatives, and the criteria have different levels of importance or weights. You may assign weights by using a pair wise comparison method, or by other means. Each cell in Figure 41 is a product of two parameters: one based on the weight of the criteria, the other represents the risk posed by the choice. Thus, in the cell at the intersection of Gamma and Potential Sales, we have 5 x 1. The weight or importance of Potential Sales is high (5), and the risk posed by Gamma (compared to others) to Potential Sales was the lowest, so it was assigned a 1. The product of the two becomes the cell value, in this case 5. Continue assigning values to all cells, and finally total each alternative. The magnitude of the total score represents the overall risk for that choice. To summarize the results, in this case, Gamma poses the highest risk, followed by Alpha.

Criteria	Weight/ Importance	Delta	Gamma	Alpha	Chi
Potential Sales	5	5x3 = 15	5x1 = 5	5x2 = 10	5x2 = 10
Regulatory Requirements	3	3x1 = 3	3x4 = 12	3x2 = 6	3x3 = 9
Skill required	2	2x2 = 4	2x3 = 6	2x4 = 8	2x4 = 8
Infrastructure required	4	4x1 = 4	4x4 = 16	4x3 = 12	4x1 = 4
Managerial support needs	1	1x4 = 4	1x2 = 2	1x2 = 2	1x4 = 4
Total:		30	41	38	35

Figure 41. Weighted Prioritization Matrix

Prioritization methods help by identifying what to work on, and do so by reducing subjectivity.

Which of the Ten Mistakes would occur if you ignored the use of Prioritization Methods?

Case Studies

Case Study 1

Technology Development and Commercialization

Background

A startup company had obtained Series I, and Series II funding. The next wave of funding hinged on the demonstration of technology readiness of the products they planned to sell. The products were based on polymer materials, and there were three competing technologies for the product, each with its unique pros and cons.

The number of discrete steps required to go from the starting raw material to product was over 120, and the company could choose from four different raw materials. Regardless of the material, the product could be based on one of the three technology platforms: A, B, or C.

The Research and Development group had completed the groundwork on all three technology platforms, and the pilot plant staff was experienced in these. However, proceeding further with all three platforms simultaneously was a cumbersome and resources draining process. It was decision time. The company had to pick between the A, B, and C platforms to pursue.

Understanding the Criteria

The criteria for evaluation of all the platforms were:

- Tests/listing and certification of product by a well recognized independent lab
- Scalability to large scale manufacturing
- Perceptions in minds of customers with regard to each platform
- Life cycle cost
- Critical dependence on "sole" supplier for one material
- Safety in use of materials within the plant
- Usability of existing equipment/processes
- Marketability of new technology platform
- Adaptability to different products (ones that would be launched within the next 3 years)

Since these criteria spanned several departments, any prioritization decisions would require involvement of multiple groups. Conflicting priorities with other projects prevented this much-needed participation, so the issue was escalated to Director level. Resolution came in about a month, and we got the right team members in place.

The team conducted a pair-wise comparison on the criteria in order to rank them by order of importance as shown in Figure 42.

		1 Test/Listing & certification of material by independent lab	2 Scalability to large scale manufacturing	3 Perceptions in minds of customers for each platform	4 Life cycle cost	5 Critical dependence on sole supplier for one material	6 Safety in use of materials	7 Usability of existing equipment/processes	8 Marketability of new technology platform	9 Adaptability to different products
1	Test/Listing & certification of material by independent lab	x	X	x	x	x	X	x	x	x
2	Scalability to large scale mfg.	1	X	x	x	x	X	x	x	x
3	Perceptions in minds of customers for each platform	3	2	x	x	x	X	x	x	x
4	Life cycle cost	4	4	4	x	x	X	x	x	x
5	Critical dependence on sole supplier for one material	1	5	3	4	x	X	x	x	x
6	Safety in use of materials	6	6	3	4	6	X	x	x	x
7	Usability of existing equipment/processes	1	7	3	4	5	6	x	x	x
8	Marketability of new technology platform	1	2	3	4	5	6	8	x	x
9	Adaptability to different products	9	9	3	4	9	6	9	8	x

Figure 42. Pair-Wise Comparison for Criteria

185

The team then created a sorted list that clearly showed which criteria were more important relative to the others. See Figure 43.

Criteria	Freq
Life cycle cost	8
Perceptions in minds of customers for each platform	6
Safety in use of materials	6
Test/Listing & certification of material by independent lab	4
Adaptability to different products	4
Critical dependence on sole supplier for one material	3
Scalability to large scale manufacturing	2
Marketability of new technology platform	2
Usability of existing equipment/processes	1

Figure 43. Criteria Sorted by Importance

The results of this analysis laid the foundation for evaluating each of the three technology platforms. The dimensions of risk in which the platforms were evaluated were:

Current Knowledge Risks This dimension was used to answer the key question of how much risk was present in each technology platform with regard to each criterion. Higher numbers meant more risk, see Figure 44.

Confidence of Meeting Requirements in the Future The team asked how well each technology platform rated against each criterion based on future trends they could currently recognize.

Current Controls The team studied what detection/preventive measures were currently in place with regard to each platform. The underlying idea was to provide for an early warning if things did not go well with regard to any of the criteria.

Using ratings on a scale of 1 to 3 and the Weighted Prioritization Matrix, the team computed the weighted totals for risk in each dimension. The matrix for Current Knowledge Risks is partially filled out. Similar matrices were prepared for the other two dimensions, however only the totals are shown in Figures 45 and 46.

Criteria	Freq	A	B	C
Life cycle cost	8	16	24	16
Perceptions in minds of customers for each platform	6	6	12	6
Safety in use of materials	6	...	...	...
Test/Listing & certification of material by independent lab	4	...	...	...
Adaptability to different products	4	...	...	...
Critical dependence on sole supplier for one material	3	...	...	...
Scalability to large scale manufacturing	2	...	...	...
Marketability of new technology platform	2	...	...	...
Usability of existing equipment/processes	1	...	...	...
Weighted Total Score		65	80	71

Figure 44. Current Knowledge Risks by Technology Platform
(Partially filled out)

	Platform		
	A	B	C
Weighted Total Score	95	48	73

Figure 45. Confidence of Meeting Requirements in Future
(Only Total Score shown)

	Platform		
	A	B	C
Weighted Total Score	69	61	86

Figure 46. Current Controls for each Technology Platform
(Only Total Score shown)

Finally, the Grand Total Weighted Score was computed by adding totals from all three dimensions (Figures 44-46), as shown in Figure 47.

	Platform		
	A	B	C
Grand Total Wtd Score	229	189	230

Figure 47. Composite Risk Score for each Technology Platform
(Sum of Totals from Figures 44-46)

This analysis segregated Option B by a wide margin. The team proposed that Platform B alone should be pursued for one more quarter. At the end of that time, they would have early indications of process capability. If it was acceptable, they could make a final decision regarding the choice of technology platform for launch.

Case Study 2

Medical Product Development - Prevention of Recall

Background

A startup company began the process of developing new technologies for reconstructive implants. This involved new materials and new designs with the potential for natural bonding with bone to provide better implant fixation. Animal studies had shown promising results, and now the development team was ready to begin human trials.

Scrutiny of the Project Plan

After coaching the executives and staff on RAMP and its benefits, the product team applied it to the project underway. The team had created a detailed project plan, and knew the key activities they needed to pursue. This project plan was to be used as the baseline to perform risk analysis.

The team clarified the definition of a successful clinical trial. Outcomes were listed, and they became the basis for identifying *failure modes* for the project. The potential *effects* from each failure mode were studied, and assigned Severity ratings. Both the *failure modes and effects* were mapped on the timeline to show when and where they would occur.

Next, the team brainstormed known and potential *causes* for each failure mode and mapped them on the same timeline. This enabled everyone to see the *causes, failure modes, and effects at a*

189

glance, together with their relationships. The team then rated each cause for Occurrence and Detection based on the current controls in the baseline project plan. As they rated the causes for Detection, they focused on the time between when the cause would occur and when it would be detected. If it could be detected, they studied the effectiveness of the current controls in place, and their time constants, which were used to estimate the Adjustment factor. The A-RPN was computed, which helped identify the most malignant causes of failure as reflected by high A-RPN values. The top five causes are listed here together with their *outcomes*.

- ❖ Inadequate strength of implant construct--*implants damaged during surgery.*
- ❖ Lack of "feel" for implant position--*implant out of place.*
- ❖ Instrument slips during use--*cuts adjacent nerve.*
- ❖ Instrument breaks during surgery-- *part of instrument left in patient.*
- ❖ Wrong size, or wrong side implant used--*joint dysfunction post operation.*

Remedial actions were defined and put into place, keeping the time constants in perspective. While compiling all the causes took some time, the risks associated with not doing such an activity were simply too high. To arrive at an acceptable risk threshold, results and performance from best similar implants and surgical procedures were studied. The A-RPN from these was estimated, and the team (together with other stake holders) set the threshold at 20% below that for the current product.

In this case study, 327 causes were identified, of which 161 were above the acceptable risk threshold. At least 22 were severe enough to cause a recall (if they were to occur).

Case Study 3

Consumer Plastic Products
Survival is not an Option

Instructions (for those familiar with the business environment in the U.S. during the 1980s and 1990s):

1. Do not read the case study in its totality. Read one section, such as the background, or one year's worth of details, and sketch out a projected timeline for the next two years. Preferably, you should use a large sheet of paper tacked to the wall and sticky notes to document each step, present and future, as you see it.

2. Identify key events as you see them on the timeline. Label them as benign or malignant. Think in terms of the *Ten Mistakes*, and identify those you see occurring.

3. Identify the PONRs for the significant events, that is, those that carry a high level of risk.

4. After you complete steps 1 – 3, read the next years' information, and update your timeline. Project one year out, and repeat steps 2 thru 4.

5. When you reach the end of the case study, answer the questions presented to you.

Instructions (for those NOT familiar with the business environment in the U.S. during the 1980s and 1990s):

1. Read the case study. Stop before the Fast Forward to 2003 section. Then start over again and go to step 2.

2. Read one section, such as the background, or one year's worth of details and sketch out a projected timeline for the next two years. Preferably, you should use a large sheet of paper tacked to the wall and sticky notes to document each step, present and future, as you see it.

3. Identify key events as you see them on the timeline. Label them as benign, or malignant. Think in terms of the *Ten Mistakes*, and identify those you see occurring.

4. Identify the PONRs for the significant events, that is, those that carry a high level of risk.

5. After you complete steps 1 – 3, read the next years' information, and update your timeline. Project one year out, and repeat steps 2 thru 4.

6. When you reach the end of the case study, answer the questions presented to you.

Background (As of 1986)

Since its inception about 17 years ago, the company CRPP (not real name) has introduced multitudes of innovative consumer plastic and rubber products that made life convenient and easier for millions in the U.S. It had a successful track record of growth and profitability that was the envy of other leading companies. The new product pipeline was loaded with innovative products

192

scheduled for launch over the next three years.

The company had tripled sales in less than ten years, and had made their brand well recognized and respected. Managers and executives at the company believed their current course to be correct. This was the scenario from early thru the mid 1980s.

Technology-wise, the barriers to entry were low; food grade plastics and molding technology were both mature areas with only marginal opportunities for differentiation. Microwave-compatible raw materials were easily available worldwide, and the industry was only moderately capital intensive. There were no special needs for factory setups as long as the risk of contamination was managed. Even that was less stringent than what is required for a food processing plant. All manufacturing was done in 5 plants located in the U.S. Midwest.

Changes on the Horizon: Observations Starting 1987

In 1987, the economy was deteriorating, interest rates and unemployment had risen in the U.S. The stock market had moderated, and then came the crash of October 1987. This soured the mood and consumer spending took a hit. Marketing managers at the company continued to supply the design and development group requirements for new products as they saw it, and the design groups continued to drive the new product development engine. The backlog of orders held steady with the book-to-bill ratio holding at 1.2.

In 1988, a new president came to the White House, this brought a brief respite from the recession. Backlog of orders kept the book-to-bill ratio around 1.2, and the market received new products with the same enthusiasm as in the past. The cashbook position was excellent, and factories ran at near full capacity. Although the larger customers increased their orders with the company, the smaller ones were beginning to turn away. Sales increased by 22 percent over the previous year because several new categories of products had been launched in the recent past. New factories were planned to meet the increasing demand, and significant capital expenses were incurred in the purchase of land for the factories. This depleted the cash at hand for the company to some extent.

In 1989, the pace of new product development continued unabated, and everyone firmly believed that this engine would keep the company going forever. The book to bill ratio dipped to 1.02, with a few complaints trickling in from the larger customers about order fill rates, accuracies, and some of the products not meeting customer's needs.

More customers were lost from the small retailers segment. In several meetings, marketing managers rationalized this as a minor blip. It should self-correct soon they opined. Besides, the smaller customers were only 7.6% of the total revenue, and the marketing managers pointed to the fact that the larger customers had been increasing their orders. The company increased their prices by an average of 2.5%.

Production ramp-up at the new factory hit a snag, with yields suffering. While not showstoppers, these snags showed gaps in logistics and production planning functions. The production managers and the general manager for worldwide operations informed the executives during a meeting that they had the problems under control. Imports of like products from China were meanwhile steadily increasing, and had doubled since 1988. However, they were barely noticeable on the shelves of the large retailers.

In 1990, a report from a well-known consumer products market research group circulated, pointing to eight competitors preparing to launch copycat products in the U.S., now that the market for such plastic products had grown. Six of the new competitors were based out of China. The Marketing group received the reports first, however it dismissed the threats as inconsequential. They rationalized that their company was too

194

strongly embedded with their distribution chain, and had a lot of new product backing, which they rationalized would maintain customer loyalty. They were confident that CRPP would not be impacted by Asian imports.

In 1991, a major customer ABC began switching to a competitor's product. This was the first blow from a large customer (customers were classified as a large customer if the revenues from them exceeded 4.5 percent of total sales). ABC cited several reasons for the switch, among which was inflexibility on the part of CRPP. The company had refused to adapt their products to what the retailer wanted in terms of colors, styles, and designs. The retailer claimed their research showed customers preferred certain colors and styles. Additionally, poor order fill rates, order inaccuracies, and continued price increases made it difficult for the retailers to offer value to their customers in what was becoming a commodity product.

The switch caused a flurry of activity in the executive suites. Sales from ABC amounted to eight percent of CRPP's revenues. The marketing group resolved very optimistically to win ABC back within two quarters. They launched a research study using graduate business students from a reputable university to determine the reasons at a deeper level.

The business students interviewed a sampling of CRPP's customers and end users. The report prepared by the students surmised: "The competitors were Chinese suppliers offering cheaper imports; spoke minimal English, and used older technology machines. Therefore, they could not be in tune with the U.S. market. The retailers would soon realize this, and be back with CRPP." The report also noted that FP a local competitor had been steadily increasing market share because they were more responsive to their customer's needs. Being a privately held company however, financial details on FP's performance could not be found.

Bolstered by the reinforcement of their hunches, the sales

force reduced the calls they were making to ABC. This led to a further decline of information exchange and by the end of 1991 ABC had switched completely. The book-to-bill ratio dropped to the mid 0.9 level, something rarely seen in the history of the company. Concerned executives knew they must take serious action soon. None of this was a secret to investors, the stock's price was reflecting this weakness in revenues and outlook. Despite this, analysts and company insiders attributed the drop to a general weakness in the market, and upcoming presidential elections next year.

Early in January 1992, a major business daily reported on the inroads being made by Chinese manufacturers in the field. The article quoted "Fueled by the revenues from ABC and smaller retailers, the Chinese manufacturers planned to triple capacity, and become a stronger force to reckon with." Their attempts at luring away more customers from CRPP grew bolder. What had initially started out as a shadowy copycat molding operation, now had a few modern factories by mid 1992. They also made plans to add a design group in-house that could take the customer's needs from concept to final product.

In July 1992, one more large retailer switched. The withdrawal of the two retailers severely hurt CRPP's sales. Their expectation to regain ABC within two quarters had proved wrong. Rationalizing their decision, they continued to maintain that it was only a matter of time before both retailers would return to them. "Wait until some of their plastics melt in the microwave, then there will be a wave of reprisals from the consumers and the Chinese competitors would be forced to make a quick exit from the U.S." they said.

They waited until the end of 1992, but none of this wishful thinking came true. More disturbing, there were indications that another retailer was eyeing suppliers in China. When this became known, serious dialog ensued in the executive offices.

The sales group pointed the finger at low order fill rates and errors in delivered products. Manufacturing and logistics indicted the marketing group, citing inaccurate forecasts that led to a build up of inventory for the wrong products. Marketing accused the design groups, saying their designs were not in tune with market's needs. The design groups denounced marketing, suggesting they did not do and adequate job of gathering the voice of the customer. Sales folks also lamented the loss of pricing power, since they had to push existing products until late in their life cycle. The blame game continued.

Pressures grew from several directions, and the board and the investment community called on the president to do something. He reluctantly pondered replacing some of his executive team. Meanwhile, all but one of the smaller retail customers had switched over to suppliers from China.

Heads had to roll, and they did. Both marketing and sales took hits. Human Resources, Manufacturing, and Quality departments were also affected as the company attempted to deal with shrinking margins because of lost sales.

When CRPP's Director of Sales asked their customers why they switched, they candidly stated, "You've been ignoring our needs for years. We have viable alternatives now, so we don't have to put up with CRPP anymore."

The sales and marketing teams considered this information too explosive to divulge to higher ups. Fearing reprisals, they withheld it from the CEO and other executives. Such comments were rarely reported from the field to those who could act on it.

The downward revision of sales and margin numbers for the following year would be the fourth in a row. The board grew impatient and concerned. They knew of situations like these, where companies were broken up, or sold off for pennies on the dollar.

In late 1993, the last of the smaller retailers switched, forcing the company again to look inside and ask some hard questions. Book to bill ratio had declined steadily, and one of the remaining four large retail chains stood on the verge of switching. If this were to happen, the company would see revenues drop to 50 percent of 1988 levels.

Four years had passed since the first symptoms of trouble (loss of customers from the smaller retailer segment) were seen. What would it take for the company to get back on sound footing? Could it happen, or was this company going the way of the automotive industry?

Fortunately, land prices had escalated significantly, so they sold land to generate much needed cash to keep the company afloat. Low utilization of the plant forced management to consider selling the new factory, but doing so would further weaken CRPP, and give a boost to competitors. Another option was to find manufacturers in China and have them manufacture products with the company's label.

Meanwhile, lower cost Chinese products continued to flood the U.S. market. The selling prices took a nosedive, and by the end of the third quarter, all of the remaining customers had asked the company to slash prices by 35 percent. The cash generated from the sale of the land could sustain the operation only through November 1994. The company had a line of credit that could help it survive for another six months, however, unless something resulted in a turnaround, further borrowing would accelerate a deteriorating condition.

Prowlers watching the scenario unfold from a distance since 1991, offered to take the company private and pay out shareholders 11 cents on the dollar. They would assume all the debt in return, and get total control of the company. Weakened to the point of being unable to negotiate a better deal, the board and the executives accepted the offer after much heated debate. New owners took control of the company starting March of 1994.

Fast Forward to 2003

The company's products still hold space on retail store shelves, but only about 20 percent of what it occupied in the early 90s. CRPPN (their new name) has diversified into building and hardware markets where margins are somewhat better, and switched to heavy use of re-cycled materials.

Now as a privately held corporation, the company's books are out of view, their financial health is therefore not known. However, customers indicate CRPPN is on the rebound. How much of the lost market it will regain is anyone's guess. Did it have to go this way? "Not at all," contend _all_ of their customers. For proof, look at FP, one of their U.S. based competitors.

NOTE: This case study is adapted from actual events. Some dates and other details have been changed to protect the identities of the parties. Company names used in the case study are not real.

Questions:

1. Can you spot which of the events were benign, and which were malignant in nature?
2. Which events and action steps had high risks?
3. What were the PONRs for the high-risk malignant events?
4. Which of the *Ten Mistakes* did you identify occurring, and where in the timeline?

Case Study 4

Business Continuity (Small Business Application)

Background

According to data provided by the British government, small businesses survive at the rate of about 75 percent after the second year, and 60 percent after the fourth year.[1] Corresponding numbers for the U.S. are 66 percent at two years, and 44 percent at four years.[2] There are about 26 million small businesses in the U.S., and these provide from 60 to 80 percent of new jobs annually. They are also responsible for a majority of the innovations that come from the U.S.[3]

An enormous disparity exists between the states (in the U.S.) with regard to the friendliness of the local governments toward small business. Hawaii, California, and District of Columbia rank near the bottom, whereas South Dakota, Nevada, and Wyoming count themselves among the top.[4]

In the backdrop of this information, I interviewed several small business owners to discuss how they manage risk in their operations. I offer one of those interviews below as an example. Conducting these interviews was of great interest to me since I have owned six small businesses over the years, both in India and the U.S. Of these six, I have used formal Risk Management methodologies in the last three with very good results.

A to Z Business Services (not their real name) provided document related services (printing, binding, scanning, storing, archiving, and disposal), to many local organizations. They had 18 staff members, including the owner. Three worked as managers/supervisors, one person doubled as the bookkeeper and front desk receptionist, and one person for sales. They used two contract employees for overflow work, and one for performing the IT function. Revenues for the last four years had grown rapidly, and last year they crossed the $2.7 million mark. The company had a line of credit for $750,000 and a bank loan of $1.02 million. Payment terms had changed over the last year, with one of their key clients going from 15 days to 30 days, and the company had to draw on the line of credit more frequently than in the past.

The accountant handled finances and provided quarterly Balance Sheet and Income Statements to Linda, the owner. Once a month, everyone came together for a staff meeting, birthday celebration, or other similar event, however, no one ever discussed business at these meetings.

During the second week of January 2006, over a lunch meeting, I asked Linda if she had conducted any Risk Management or Business Continuity Planning for her operation. She gave me a skeptical smile and said, "I can't worry myself with *'What ifs.'* Taking risks is a part of life and unavoidable." Knowing that most small business owners live with such paradigms (which land them in avoidable trouble), I followed up with another question. "So, what happens if you can't work for 4 weeks, and the staff can't communicate with you for some reason? Don't say anything. Just write down what would happen to and in your business."

After she finished, I asked her why she wrote the ones she did, and to describe the *consequences* of each. Here is what she said:

1   Payroll will be held up – *may lose employees.*
2   Payments to suppliers will be delayed – *unhappy suppliers and possibly some penalties imposed.*
3   Customers will not be served properly – *loss of good will with some customers, one customer may be permanently lost.*

201

4   Depending on the month, tax payments may be delayed – *incurring penalties.*
5   Critical decisions may be delayed – *loss of future business.*
6   Not seeing her around – *employees would be un-nerved.*
7   Managers and supervisors will be uncomfortable with some of the decisions they may face – *adding to more chaos.*

She indicated these were the ones that had occurred in the last six months, or she remembered them because they were painful. Seeing the consequences on paper made her uneasy. She said, "Thanks for a dose of insomnia, what solutions can you offer?"

I could see her discomfiture. "Well, you can succeed in your business by choice or by chance. The choice is yours to make Linda. A failure to foresee and act pro-actively leads to more dependence on luck. Like most small business owners, you were in your comfort zone until these risks surfaced. You were already committing one of the mistakes I've discussed in my book. There are nine other mistakes that people often make with regard to Risk Management. Of these, I just noticed two more – Recency and Frequency, and The Terribility Factor." I paused to see if she was interested in hearing more.

She said, "I'd like to know more, but I expect you to show me how I can become risk free as well."

Sensing she was expecting paradise, I had to let her know that there is no such thing as being risk free. Some amount of risk will always exist. However, we can learn more about prudent risk taking, which leads to sounder decisions and actions. I can't provide you a failure proof guarantee, but I can offer you a method to identify the risks you face in your business, and means for managing the same. I could tell she was eager to get started.

We began with a review of the *Ten Mistakes*, but before I could finish, she picked up on the *Iceberg* and interrupted me.

"Why do I feel I am looking at just the tip of the iceberg?"

202

"If this is the first time you're conducting Risk Analysis in your business, that's to be expected," I replied. "It will be far more constructive if we can go off-site for three days, a half day at a time, to study the whole picture. You'll need your key staff to participate as well."

"What would we get out of it?" she asked.

"You'll get a comprehensive view of the risks your business faces; a listing of the sources of the risks; and the order of priority for addressing these."

"And the corrective actions?" she asked.

"These should come from you and your staff after you identify the risks and their sources, which will be most likely about four to five weeks from now. Deployment of the mitigation efforts may take some time. But, as of today, you don't even have a good sense of the potential risks that lurk out there."

She accepted the suggestion, and three weeks later, we found ourselves at the off-site location.

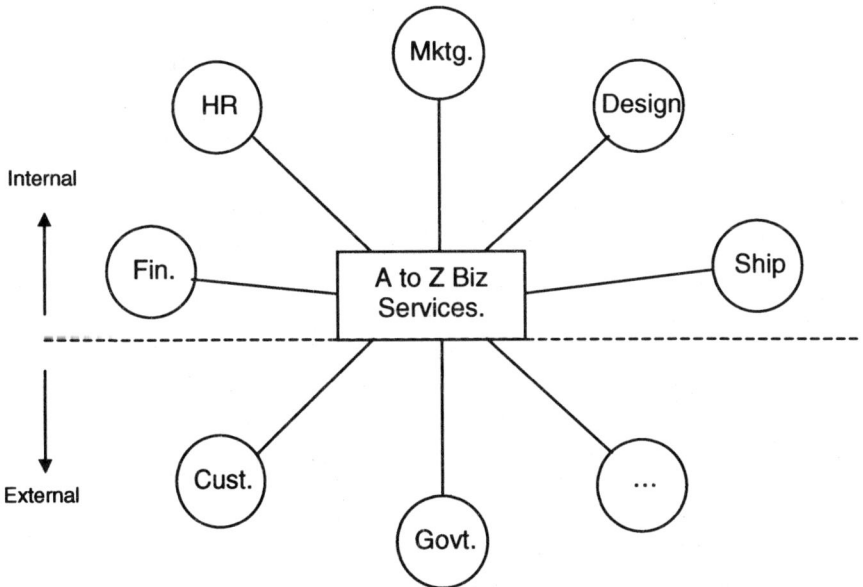

Figure 48. A to Z Business - 360° View

The Offsite Summit

We began the day with introductions and icebreakers, and then quickly got down to business. First, we simply identified sources of risk from the different facets of the organization, and from external sources as shown in Figure 48.

They identified nine sources of risk: Government and Regulations, Infrastructure, Customers, Production, Human Resources, Shipping, Marketing and Sales, Accounting Finance, and Scheduling. While some of these facets had dedicated resources to perform the function, others had shared resources.

Because risk is abstract in nature, it proved hard to tackle. The staff knew it exists in everything, and is present everywhere all the time. "How do we even make sense of risk, and, where do we start?" asked one of their managers.

Seeing the team stymied, I suggested they begin by focusing on the outputs from the organization by putting A to Z in the center, and thinking about what does it do? Drawing a simple input output diagram as shown in Figure 49 got them started. They worked on what were the outputs, and who were the users of the same? As this exercise continued, they created a list of 46 outputs, some very clear, others hazy such as goodwill generated.

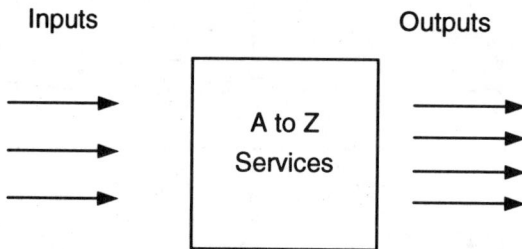

Inputs   Outputs

A to Z
Services

Figure 49. Inputs and Outputs for A to Z Services

Each of these 46 outputs could produce a failure. They easily understood this and saw where they were headed now.

They also built a Process/Event Map to layout how the

organization worked. This turned out to be an exciting activity as it was the first time they created such a map. Many hidden assumptions and interdependencies surfaced which were either addressed immediately or tabled for future investigation. A side benefit was realizing there was about 12% redundant work that occurred in their business. It was decided to eliminate that, resulting in a quick win of productivity gains.

Focusing on each failure mode to identify corrective action during the summit was impractical, instead, the team estimated the RPN for a few and prioritized them. We found an additional 18 failure modes as we examined the process map. From the 65 risks that had been identified now they had to choose one that represented a threshold level, something they would consider an acceptable operational risk.

They identified five risks as follows:

- The one with the highest RPN
- The one with the lowest RPN
- The one in the middle
- One that lies between the middle and the lowest RPN
- One that lies between the middle and the highest RPN

This spectrum made it easier for them to come up with a threshold level, which they set at 350 on a scale of 1 to 1000. Fifteen risk factors stood below this level, and 50 were above. I've listed the top seven here:

1. Insufficient cash flow can result in the company's bankruptcy.
2. Risk of injury to visitors/personnel as they try to enter or exit the building.
3. A key customer switches to work with another supplier.
4. New competitor (national chain) comes to town.
5. Bank calls up on the business loan and asks to retire it

ahead of time.

6. Unprepared to deal with fire hazard in the building.
7. Missed delivery deadlines to customers.

The Process and Event maps identified a few early indicators that existed in the operations to warn about any of the high-risk situations. After we completed the RAMP approach, the team realized what they needed to do. They identified PONRs for each of the causes that lead to high RPN failure modes, which gave them a new sense of direction and reinforced the fact that Risk Management activities needed to continue on a regular basis.

Figure 50 shows a partial list of the corrective actions they put in place (they are extracted from the spreadsheet used in the exercise).

Risk to Business	Cause or Causes	Corrective/Preventive Actions
1 – Cash flow – can result in the company's premature bankruptcy	Payment delays from the customers - no tracking of whether the invoices are in their system or not.	Confirm invoices are in the A/P system of the customer.
2 – Risk of injury to visitors/personnel as they try to enter/exit the building	Steps too high at entrance from parking lot on to the sidewalk	Install railing to prevent visitors using the steps, guide them to the end of the sidewalk where access to sidewalk is better and safer
	The second entrance door has clear glass which is invisible (causing people to bump into it)	Install a handle with brass backing plate to ensure it is obvious that one has to push on the door to open it.

206

Risk to Business	Cause or Causes	Corrective/Preventive Actions
3 – A key customer switches - to work with another supplier	Delayed shipments, lower prices offered by competitors	Ensure the price of the service provided is kept at reasonable levels (benchmarking). Begin tracking cycle time for orders from the day the order is placed by the customer to the time it is completed. Establish baseline, and then look for opportunities to improve.
4 – New competitor (national chain) comes to town	Hard to say what can be the cause here - may be they think this would be a profitable venture for them	Build stronger relationships with existing customers, and expand customer base aggressively by networking through chamber of commerce. Reorganize/re-group the staff into account teams for customers. Then ensure everyone in the account team knows each customer, and their priorities, likes, dislikes, etc. Keep track of new businesses opening up.
5 – Bank calls up on the business loan – and asks to retire it ahead of time	Begin slipping on monthly payments, low cash position	Work to ensure that we are not drawing on the Line of Credit; use it only as reserve. Use the "Dry Well Time" concept as suggested by Rai on a monthly basis - rather than using the P&L statements, or Balance Sheets
6 – Ill prepared to deal with fire hazard in the building	Huge stacks of boxes with paper documents (customer's records) in several rooms. Fire extinguishers are centrally located. Fire detection alarms missing.	Re-locate fire extinguishers and increase to two per room. Install fire detection alarms. Add funds to install automatic sprinkler systems in next year's budget.
7 – Missed delivery deadlines to customers	More than 2 production (from any functional unit) staff fall sick on a given day	Cross train employees, increase on call contract labor from 2 to 3

Risk to Business	Cause or Causes	Corrective/Preventive Actions
	Incorrect orders taken from customers, and or over optimistic commitments made	Initiate regular business meetings/updates between functional groups. Sales to be made aware of capabilities and limitations of production departments. Begin using "indicators" for production system operational level for each area.
	Equipment breakdowns (scanner, software based glitches, Level II and higher order copier malfunctions...)	Get 1 person trained and certified in carrying out repairs/trouble shooting on key production equipment, instead of waiting for factory technicians all the time.
	Materials run short (binding supplies, gold/silver foil, etc.)	Change layout of storage areas, add visual indicators (yellow cards) for alerting of low inventory

Figure 50. Top Seven Risks and their Resolution for A to Z Services

Closing comments by the owner

"While this was not rocket science, it was by far the most valuable exercise I've been through. Even my Fortune 100 employer that I left six years ago didn't have their act together this well. I now realize how much we had left to chance."

How many of these are common to the 13 common causes of business failures listed in Chapter 7?

Case Study 5

Continue Product on Market or Pull Back

Background

Among the worst specters that haunt companies is the fear of having to recall a product. Often what starts out as an occasional complaint (remember Firestone tires in the U. S.?) later snowballs into a major product controversy! Once a critical mass of the populace is convinced that a product is flawed, truth doesn't matter anymore. It takes quite some time for the public to forget the event and return to buying the same product, provided no other mishaps occur in the meanwhile.

Take the example of Audi 5000. During the 1980s, nearly 1800 incidents of sudden acceleration were reported and the company chose to blame it on drivers inadvertently stepping on the accelerator.[5] The company lost 80 percent of its market share during the 1980s. Today, few remember the issue with the Audi brand, and many hold it in high regard again.

A similar scenario unfolded with a medical device manufacturer. The company had grown very aggressively in a new market, and recently crossed $69 million in sales. Acquired by a Fortune 100 corporation, the manufacturer had a remarkable record of bringing great medical products to market. Recently however, there had been isolated reports of field incidents. Some had to do with the migration of the implant inside the body, others reported loosening which eventually resulted in pain and a return to pre-implant conditions. The regulatory environment requires the company to report every such finding to the FDA, and it was now concerned about the cases that might arise in the future. *The company's staff were aware of the Tip of the Iceberg mistake.*

The Customer Service Manager assembled key staff members who were trained in Risk Management to discuss a resolution to these complaints. Her concern was that, after the acquisition by the Fortune 100 Corporation, theirs was not a small company any more, and therefore could be considered a high value target.

Defensive Measures Begin with Trepidation

After heated debate over the need for launching an internal probe, management assembled a cross-functional team, which included professionals and engineers from design, manufacturing, supplier quality, regulatory affairs, marketing, sales, and distribution. The team studied the Design History Files together with the Risk Analysis that had been conducted when the product was designed and initially released.

A two-page FMEA document listed eleven failures, and their associated risks. The causes were identified, and RPN had been calculated. How the risks would be addressed was also indicated in the document. The team suspected that in this case the *Tip of the Iceberg* mistake had already been committed. Why? Because the risks identified came from the narrow perspective of the product design group only.

360° Risk Identification

First, the team created a 360° map of all the areas that impacted the product, as shown in Figure 51. Many of these areas were not represented on the team, so with some effort an extended team of subject matter experts was identified.

Material
flow
Internal and
External

Complaints
and returns

VOC / User
needs
1 Surgeon
2 Hospital
3...

Field
Service

Existing
Product

Regulatory
Affairs

Financial
results

Testing,
Evaluation
and
Reliability

Design and
development

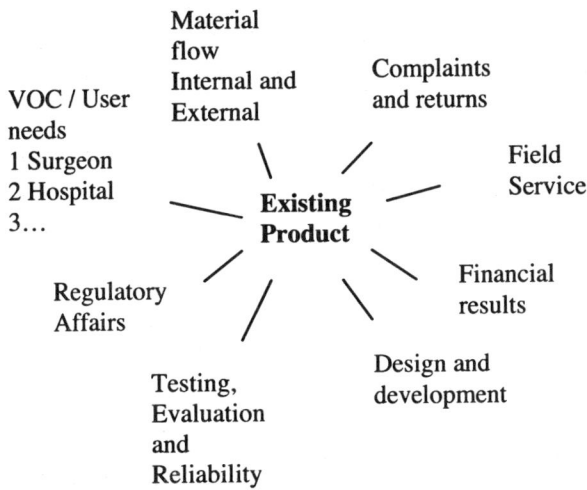

Figure 51. 360° Areas of Impact

Next, the inputs and outputs from each area were defined as they pertained to the product in question. An example (partial listing) of this is shown in Figure 52. This provided the team a clear perspective of the outputs from each area, and therefore which failure modes might occur.

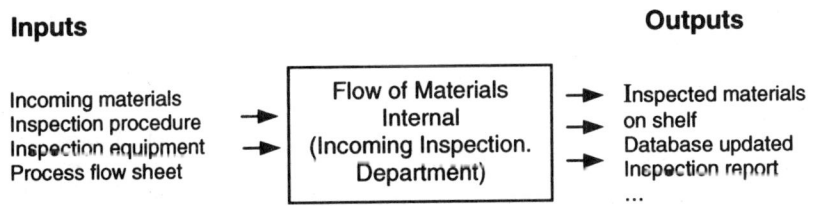

Inputs   **Outputs**

Incoming materials
Inspection procedure
Inspection equipment
Process flow sheet

Flow of Materials
Internal
(Incoming Inspection.
Department)

Inspected materials
on shelf
Database updated
Inspection report
...

Figure 52. Inputs and Outputs by Area

One of the failure modes from Incoming Inspection Department would be that discrepant materials go on shelf for use. Figure 53 lists additional failure modes. In all, 197 failure modes were thus identified with the causes running into 400+ line items.

211

Of these 197 failure modes, approximately 84 percent were found to be above the acceptable risk threshold. The team presented the report to the executive management of the company despite concerns that the messenger would invite their wrath. At first, the executives expressed disbelief. How could the product team overlook more than 90% of the issues they asked. This happens in many companies, due to the overwhelming pressure to produce results. Since the risk analysis was a product of the expertise from within the company, it stood its ground.

RPN*	Failure Mode	Source of Risk	Identified by previous Risk Analysis?	Current Control Identified per Internal Documents/Procedures	S	O	D	Comments/Notes
100	Wrong materials used for Implant	Supplier	No	None	5	4	5	Vendor does not have means to verify materials
16	Discrepant parts put on out going shelf	Inspection Dept. operations	No	002 – 2902	4	2	2	Clearly marked areas, and procedure exist
16	Incorrect entry into database	Inspection Dept	No	002-2902, and Supplier Procedures	4	2	2	Bar-coding of all parts shipped by supplier
27	Inspection report in error	Inspection Dept.	No	002-2902	3	3	3	Too many areas where Inspectors have to enter information

*Computed from the product of Severity, Occurrence, and Detection

Figure 53. Failure Modes - Incoming Inspection Department
(Partial listing)

212

At the last communication, the company was mulling over a decision on their next steps, however they now had better information on which to base a decision. Additionally, this analysis could be used as the foundation for a whole family of products on the drawing board. Now they had a vaccine to immunize themselves against the virus of ignoransk (ignorance + risk)!

In May 2006, as I continued to work on this book, I happened to study Michael Cabbage's book, *Comm Check,* on the final flight of Columbia. On page 205 I read, "The program's critical items list tracks almost 5400 potential hazards in an effort to manage and control the risk. Some 4222 (78 percent) are listed as 'Criticality 1/1R.' The failure of a Criticality 1 item could result in the loss of the shuttle and it's crew." At the time of Columbia's launch, 3233 of the criticality 1/1R items had some sort of a waiver. A third of those waivers had not been reviewed in more than a decade.

This is more evidence that our species tends to ignore about 80% of the risks. Chance takes over in these cases, and when problems occur we are surprised. Statements such as "It was an accident" provide a convenient escape, and we doom ourselves to making the same mistake again! You will recall from the Introduction that only 8% of the people believed a fire alarm when it went off.

Case Study 6

Business Continuity – Wake Up Call After PONR
(Medium Size Public Company)

Background

This case study relates the story of a company listed on the NASDAQ, the premier stock exchange in the U.S. A producer of technology products, it had seen a precipitous decline in stock price over nine months, going from over $20 to under $8, a loss of 60 percent. During the same period, the exchange index rose by approximately 3 percent.

As a result, the company came under severe pressure and scrutiny from analysts who constantly called the company. The president was inundated with questions and requests for interviews. The lenders were also on edge. Those within the company believed that the problems stemmed from internal causes related to missed product launches and the inability of the company to correct problems in existing products.

The previous year, the company had over 1600 employees working in design, manufacturing, development, research, marketing, sales, human resources, finance, customer service, supplier development/management, and information technology. Three rounds of layoffs had occurred, and the head count stood just shy of 900 today.

One of the senior directors contacted me to help the organization understand the causes, to work with the executive team for a turnaround, and to instill Business Excellence together with use of Risk Management throughout the company.

I had my first meeting with the senior director and the executive VP during Month 0 (we will use this as the reference starting point.). They indicated this was urgent and required resolution rather quickly. We had to start the analysis early in Month 2, and be complete by the end of Month 3. The idea was to have an unbiased third party review their operations and present their analysis and findings in the form of a report. This would take approximately five man-weeks of effort. After careful study and deliberation, these findings could be used to identify future steps the company needed to take. Work on next year's operating plans was to begin in Month 5.

In a scoping meeting, we outlined the approximate timetable. We were to have the first working session to create the statement of work early in Month 1. The date for the working meeting was to be decided soon.

Readers may recall I had suggested that we should maintain a Log Book as an antidote? It was done for this case study, as shown in Figure 54, Weekly Log of Events after the Scoping Meeting starting next page.

See if you can spot some of the *Ten Mistakes* as they happen. Also, identify the current controls and PONRs as you go. Think about the antidotes we discussed earlier in the book. Which antidote would you use and when?

Weekly Log of Events after the Scoping Meeting

Month/ Week	Activity Description	Outcome /Response	Which of the Ten Mistakes occurred? Which Antidote would work?	Observations/ Notes
1/1	Call to set date and time for first working session	Sr. Director has not yet visited with the Executive VP to pick a date		Stock price hovers around $7 to $8
1/2	Request for firm date to conduct first working session	Executive VP will be out for 2 weeks, will pick a date in fourth week		Online message boards show many posts criticizing the company, while some defend the company
1/4	Request for firm date for first working session	Will discuss with executive staff and get back next week		Company makes a layoff announcement; stock moves up by $0.30 cents to about $6.50
2/1	Call to check on outcomes of executive staff meeting. Alerted them my logs show no progress in four weeks.	The risk analysis is a "go". First working session will happen in 2 weeks		Business media reports indicate heavy insider selling of stock over the last 4 months
2/2				Analysts question company operations.
2/3	Call to check on date set. Inform Sr. Director available window for Risk Analysis is closing in. Alerted them – no progress in 6 weeks	Learned that the Sr. Director and one executive will be on sabbatical for the next 6 weeks.		Executives tell media they will turn the company around. 43 people laid off; one product line shut down. Message board activity is highest ever.

Month/ Week	Activity Description	Outcome /Response	Which of the Ten Mistakes occurred? Which Antidote would work?	Observations/ Notes
2/4				Stock drops below $6.50 level, a new 52 week low
3/2				Press release indicates new contracts won from a leading telecom equipment provider
3/3				Analysts question if the contracts will be much help
3/4				Stock drops below $6. Announcement in media indicates company seeking to raise debt to stay afloat
4/2	Check with Sr. Director on dates again. Raise concern over delays again.	Just returned from sabbatical, will check with executive VP and get back next week		
2/3	Call to check if date is set. Inform Sr. available window to do Risk Analysis is closing in. Alerted them – no pro-gress in 6 weeks	Learned that the Sr. Director and one of the executives will be on sabbatical for the next 6 weeks.		Sr. Director and executive VP tell media they will turn the company around. 43 people are laid off, one product line is shut down. Message board activity is high.

217

Month/ Week	Activity Description	Outcome /Response	Which of the Ten Mistakes occurred? Which Antidote would work?	Observations/ Notes
2/4				Stock drops below $6.50 level, a new 52 week low
3/2				Press release from the company indicates new contracts from a leading equipment provider
3/3				Analysts question if the contracts will be much help
3/4				Stock drops below $6. Announcement in media indicates company seeking to raise debt to stay afloat
4/2	Check with Sr. Director on dates again. Raise concern over delays again.	Just returned from sabbatical, will check with executive VP and get back next week		
4/3	Inform Sr. Director we will not have enough time before Month 5 to do the Risk Analysis.			President resigns, stock drops by $0.66.

Month/ Week	Activity Description	Outcome /Response	Which of the Ten Mistakes occurred? Which Antidote would work?	Observations/ Notes
4/4	Inform Sr. Director the window has passed, and any work started now will go into Month 6	Willing to re-scope the timeline and get the Purchase Order started		Stock dips below $5 but recovers. Flurry of calls from analysts, and investors. Message boards rife with rumors of bankruptcy
5/2	Check on status of Purchase Order	Sr. Director is out of town, request has been passed on to Purchasing department		Private investor group expresses in buying the company. Options activity is very high
5/3	Check on status of Purchase Order	It is in progress we are told		
5/4	Write to Sr. Director and Executive VP that even the re-scoped timeline is not workable	Operating plan drawn up with educated guesses. They believe they know the causes		
6/1	End follow up			
6/3				Executive VP resigns

Figure 54. Log of Events after Scoping Meeting

Case Study 7

Reactive Gas Delivery System Analysis

Background

Semiconductor chips are used in just about every product today and these chips are getting quite sophisticated. The advanced chips require extremely fine circuits, which cannot be produced by wet chemical processing. Therefore, reactive gases are used for this purpose. This case study is based on a gas delivery system used in chip manufacturing industry. A product team responsible for this system performed the analysis.

The team followed the *Systematic Approach* earlier defined as *RAMP*. Since the first two steps were already done, they started with step 3 *"Define the Inputs and Outputs for the Object"* and followed the Tops Down approach.

Overall function of the system

The system had 14 outputs and 32 inputs, three of each are shown in Figure 55. A partial block diagram with elements of the system is shown in Figure 56.

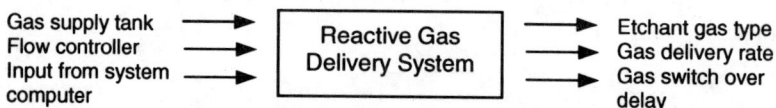

Gas supply tank
Flow controller
Input from system computer
→ Reactive Gas Delivery System →
Etchant gas type
Gas delivery rate
Gas switch over delay

Figure 55. Gas Delivery System Input Output Diagram (Partial)

220

Depending on the circuitry to be produced on the chip, one or more etchant gases would be needed in a finely controlled volume and rate. Before gas switchovers occurred, the system was required to be purged, which was accomplished by flushing out the system with Argon gas. The gases were stored in tanks, and piped into a manifold where they were mixed with other gases if needed. These were then delivered to a process chamber where the wafers were processed.

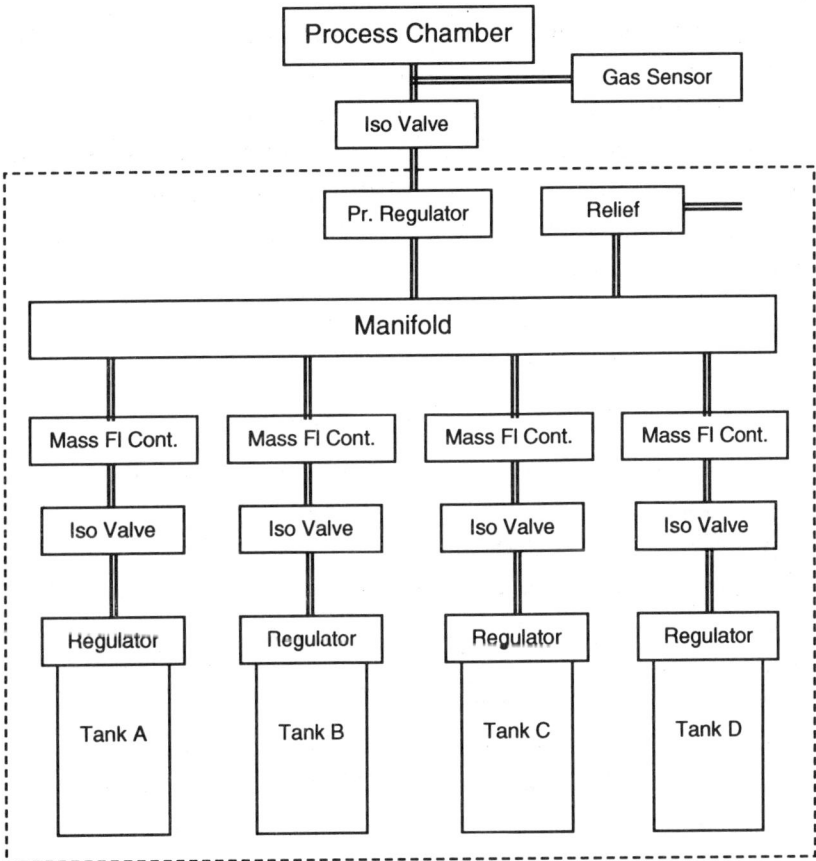

Figure 56. Block Diagram showing elements of Gas Delivery System (Scope of analysis defined by dotted lines)

Conducting Risk Analysis

Working with the Tops Down approach, the team used the outputs to identify failure modes for the Gas Delivery System. Effects were attributed to what would happen at the Chamber if a failure were to occur. Causes were traced to the elements within the Gas Delivery System or the inputs to the system. Figure 58 shows the complete analysis for one failure mode. This was repeated for each of the 14 failure modes.

The team identified the highest A-RPN causes and determined the corrective actions for the same. As part of this step, the team used Event Maps as shown in Figure 57. Initially, each event was listed on a sticky note and put on the wall for everyone to see. Then they were re-arranged to reflect the sequence, and align with the respective functional group. Once this was done, the event map could be studied easily.

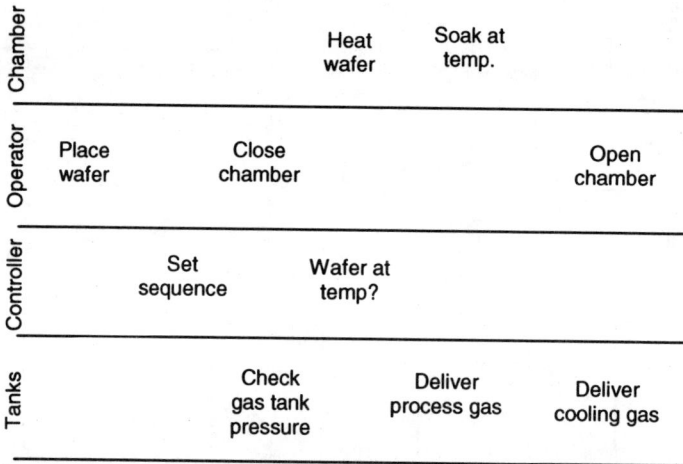

Chamber			Heat wafer	Soak at temp.		
Operator	Place wafer		Close chamber			Open chamber
Controller		Set sequence		Wafer at temp?		
Tanks			Check gas tank pressure	Deliver process gas		Deliver cooling gas

Figure 57. Event Map for Reactive Gas Delivery System

222

The team then identified what corrective action would be implemented, and where (accounting for the time constant) on the event map.

#	Failure	Why (Cause)	O	Worst Case Effect of Failure	S	Controls	D	Time const.	Adj	A-RPN
1	Gas delivery rate too high	Tank regulator setting incorrect	3	Excessive flow into chamber	8	Mass Fl Contr	3	At or after PONR	10	720
2		Mass Fl Contr. Defective	5		8	None	10		10	4000
3		Wrong input signal	2		8	None	10		10	1600
4		Incorrect recipe selected	6		8	Color coded recipe #s	5		10	2400
5	Gas delivery rate too low	Tank pressure too low	4	Low flow into chamber	3	Mass Fl Contr	3		10	360
6		Tank regulator setting incorrect	3		3	Mass Fl Contr	3		10	270
7		Mass Fl Contr. Defective	5		3	None	10		10	1500
8		Wrong input signal	2		3	None	10		10	600
9		Incorrect recipe selected	6		3	Color coded recipe #s	5		10	900

Figure 58. Risk Analysis on Reactive Gas Delivery System
Traditional FMEA Form used with Adjustment Factor
(Showing Failure Modes related to Gas Delivery Rate)

Concluding Comments on Case Studies

Case studies discussed here were selected from over 100 that were completed during the last 20 years. In many instances convincing the stakeholders to initiate risk analysis was the hardest part; however, once they started, the inertia waned. The metaphor that helped me convince them was, "If you are already in debilitating pain (or dysfunctional), and some medication can alleviate it, what is the harm in trying some?" Invariably, at the end they realized the value it had to offer, and wondered why they did not start earlier. Yet, there will be some procrastinators who just want to stay put.

Learning from those experiences, I developed another technique to get them going. In this case, *they* evaluate the benefits of change and the cost of doing nothing. Then I drew their attention to how they can pro-actively manage risk, to ensure their success. I trust you will find the methods useful, and wish you success as you use the methods outlined here.

If you would like to make suggestions or submit a case study for inclusion in future editions of the book, please e-mail me at: rai_chowdhary@yahoo.com.

Sources:
1. http://www.sbs.gov.uk/SBS_Gov_files/researchandstats/VATSurvivalRates 1994-2003.xls#'Table 8 Extended UK'!A1
2. http://www.smallbusinessnotes.com/aboutsb/sbfacts/sbsurvival.html
3. http://www.score.org/small_biz_stats.html
4. http://www.sbsc.org/Media/pdf/SBSI_2004.pdf#search=%22small%20busi ness%20survival%20rates%22
5. http://www.autosafety.org/article.php?did=22&scid=41

About the Author

Rai Chowdhary is an award winning speaker, author, business coach, and entrepreneur. He was born in Bombay, India, and now lives near Austin, Texas. He is the founder of TEAM 2000, a training and coaching firm that provides services worldwide. His education includes Mechanical, and Production Engineering, Business Management, and a Masters in Materials Science. He is a Certified Quality Engineer, Quality Manager, and Six Sigma Black Belt. He serves on the ISO Technical Committee 223 for Societal Risk Management, and was an examiner for the Texas Award for Performance Excellence.

Over 20,000 participants from government and industry have attended Rai's seminars and workshops. Some of the organizations he has worked with include Abbott Spine, ActivePower, Amedica, Applied Materials, Celerity, Dell, Encore Medical, Federation of Indian Chambers of Commerce and Industry (FICCI), Larsen and Toubro, Lexmark, National Center for Quality Management, National Thermal Power Commission, Quality Council of India, Teco Westinghouse, and associations such as Austin Contact Center Alliance, ISO 9000 Institute, Round Rock Chamber of Commerce, Salt Lake City Chamber of Commerce, American Society for Quality (Austin, and Dallas), APICS (Austin, and Santa Clara), The Indus Entrepreneurs (TiE), and National Society for Professional Engineers (NSPE).

To order additional copies of
Ten Mistakes of Risk Management

Name_____

Address _____

_____

_____

$19.95 x _____ copies = _____

Sales Tax _____
(Texas residents add 8.25% sales tax)

Please add $3.50 postage and handling _____

Total amount due: _____

Please send check or money order for books to:

TEAM 2000
8760A, Research Blvd., #418
Austin, TX 78758

Or
Visit us at
www.hownwhy.com
To schedule a seminar/workshop on 'Risk Management please call:
TEAM 2000 at (512) 244-9712,
or send an e-mail to info@www.hownwhy.com